Ettinger Law Firm's Guide to Protecting Your Future

Michael Ettinger
Attorney and Counselor at Law

Member: Elder and Special Needs Law; Trusts and Estates Law; and Senior Lawyers Sections of The New York State Bar Association

Copyright © 2023 by Michael Ettinger

All rights reserved. No part of this book shall be reproduced, stored in a retrieval system, or transmitted by any means, electronic, mechanical, photocopying, recording, or otherwise, without written permission from the publisher. No patent liability is assumed with respect to the use of the information contained herein. Although every precaution has been taken in the preparation of this book, the publisher and author assume no responsibility for errors or omissions. Neither is any liability assumed for damages resulting from the use of information contained herein. For information, address Ettinger Law Firm, 125 Wolf Road, Albany, New York 12205.

Disclaimer: This publication contains the opinions and ideas of its author. It is intended to provide helpful and informative materials on the subject matter covered. It is sold with the understanding that the author and publisher are not engaged in rendering professional services in the book. If the reader requires personal assistance or advice, a competent professional should be consulted.

The author and publisher specifically disclaim any responsibility for any liability, loss, or risk, personal or otherwise, which is incurred as a consequence, directly or indirectly, of the use and application of any of the contents of this book.

Ettinger Law Firm may be contacted by phone at 800-500-2525 or email at info@trustlaw.com.

Cover photo by: Michael Ettinger
Amelia Island, Florida

Attorney advertising

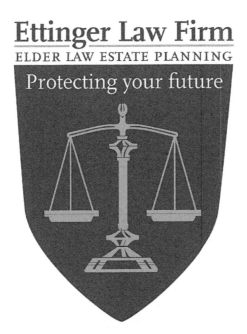

Acknowledgements

I would like to acknowledge the love and support of my dear spouse and law partner, Suzanne Ettinger, whose poise and good sense have helped to propel the growth of Ettinger Law Firm – not merely in size, but more significantly, in the grace and dignity we endeavor to bring to each client and their precious matter.

Any enterprise is no more than the sum of the people working in it and, to that end, I am deeply indebted to the caring people who labor every day to make Ettinger Law Firm the very best it can be in service to the public.

A special thanks to Patricia Brown, Director of Client Relations at Ettinger Law Firm, for her enormous contribution to making this book a reality as well as for her exemplary service to myself, the law firm and its clients for over thirty years.

Acknowledgements

My final acknowledgement is to my dear late mother, Sylvia Perlman Lesser, from who I learned, in retrospect, that the greatest blessing in life is a good mother. Thank you mom for so much but most of all for teaching me that the purpose of life is to live joyously.

Contents

INTRODUCTION

ELDER LAW ESTATE PLANNING

Chapter 1	What is Elder Law Estate Planning	9
Chapter 2	Pitfalls of Will Planning	15
Chapter 3	The Five Steps to an Elder Law Estate Plan	19
Chapter 4	The Two Biggest Mistakes in Planning	31
Chapter 5	Components of an Elder Law Estate Plan	35
Chapter 6	Inheritance Protection Trusts (IPT)	41
Chapter 7	Powers of Attorney	43
Chapter 8	Health Care Decision-Making	47
Chapter 9	Special Needs Trusts (SNT)	51
Chapter 10	Trusts for Minor Grandchildren	55
Chapter 11	Second Marriage Planning	57

Chapter 12	Planning for Those Without Children	61
Chapter 13	Protecting Assets for Spendthrift Children	65
Chapter 14	Planning for Same-Sex Couples	69
Chapter 15	Planning Issues for Women	73
Chapter 16	Disinheriting A Spouse	79
Chapter 17	Avoiding Guardianship in New York	81
Chapter 18	Business Succession Planning	83
Chapter 19	Prenuptial Agreements	87
Chapter 20	Contesting a Will	91
Chapter 21	The Young Family Estate Plan (YFEP)	93

FINANCIAL AND TAX ASPECTS OF ESTATE PLANNING

Chapter 22	The SECURE Act and Your IRA	99
Chapter 23	Leaving an IRA to a Trust	101
Chapter 24	Tax Issues on Death	103
Chapter 25	Disclaimer Trusts for Taxable Estates	105
Chapter 26	New York and Federal Estate Taxes	107
Chapter 27	Mistakes with Beneficiary Designations	109
Chapter 28	Income Taxation of Trusts	111
Chapter 29	Capital Gains Tax Tips	113
Chapter 30	Cashing in Your Life Insurance	115
Chapter 31	Reverse Mortgages	117

THE SOCIAL SIDE OF ESTATE PLANNING

Chapter 32	Good Reasons to Plan Your Estate	123
Chapter 33	Leaving a Family Business	127
Chapter 34	Estate Planning for the Estranged Child	129
Chapter 35	Don't Wait for Something to Happen	133
Chapter 36	Celebrity Estate Planning Mistakes	135
Chapter 37	Social Costs in Estate Planning	139
Chapter 38	Planning For and Executing Inheritances	141
Chapter 39	Writing an Ethical Will	145
Chapter 40	Planning for Those You Are Responsible For	147
Chapter 41	Leaving a Vacation Home to Family	149
Chapter 42	Using "Moral Suasion" in Estate Planning	151
Chapter 43	The Attorney-Client Relationship	153
Chapter 44	The Privilege to Serve	155
Chapter 45	Life Stories Preserved	157
Chapter 46	Donating Your Body to Science	159

MEDICAID PLANNING STRATEGIES

Chapter 47	Protecting Assets with Caregiver Agreements	165
Chapter 48	Medicaid Asset Protection Trusts (MAPT)	169
Chapter 49	Seven Myths About MAPT's	177
Chapter 50	Home Care with Community Medicaid	181
Chapter 51	Long-Term Care Insurance v. MAPT	185

Chapter 52	Applying for Medicaid	187
Chapter 53	Medicaid Exempt Assets	191
Chapter 54	Medicaid Annuities to Protect Assets	195
Chapter 55	Spousal Refusal - "Just Say No"	197
Chapter 56	Saving Half on the Nursing Home Doorstep	201

ESTATE ADMINISTRATION UPON DEATH

Chapter 57	Estate Administration and Probate	207
Chapter 58	Trustee's Duties Upon Death	215
Chapter 59	Using Professional Trustees	221

HEALTH AND WELL-BEING FOR OLDER ADULTS

Chapter 60	Keeping the Lights On	227
Chapter 61	Accepting What Is	229
Chapter 62	The Caregiver as the Invisible Patient	231
Chapter 63	Elder Abuse	233
Chapter 64	Positive Aspects of Aging	235
Chapter 65	Book Review: "Healthy at 100" by John Robbins	237
Chapter 66	Polypharmacy in Older Adults	241
Chapter 67	Better Sleep for Older Adults	243
Chapter 68	Death with Dignity: Hospice Care	245
Chapter 69	Aging Life Care Managers: ALCM	247
Chapter 70	Book Review: "Happiness is a Choice You Make" by John Leland	251

Contents

Chapter 71	Battling the Epidemic of Loneliness	251
Chapter 72	Health Benefits of Forgiveness	253
Chapter 73	Book Review: "Let's Talk About Death" by Michael Hebb	255
Chapter 74	Strength Training for Seniors	257
Chapter 75	Book Review: "Successful Aging" by Daniel J. Levitin	259
Chapter 76	Book Review: "Die with Zero" by Bill Perkins	261
Chapter 77	Book Review: "The Good Life" by Robert Waldinger, MD and Marc Schulz, PhD	263
Chapter 78	Increasing Your Emotional Intelligence	265
Chapter 79	Multivitamins and Older Adults	267
Chapter 80	Book Review: "Outlive: The Science & Art of Longevity" by Peter Attia, MD	269
Chapter 81	The Attitude of Gratitude	273
Chapter 82	Book Review: "Flourish" by Martin E. P. Seligman	277
Chapter 83	The Scourge of Ageism	283

APPENDIX: ABOUT ETTINGER LAW FIRM

Chapter 1	The Ettinger Elder Law Estate Planning Process	289
Chapter 2	Features of Our Practice	293
Chapter 3	The Ettinger Law Firm Way	295

Introduction

The title of this book reflects our law firm's logo "Protecting Your Future", a concept which reflects the essence of what we do (1) having a plan for disability both as to who will be in charge and how your assets will be protected and (2) how your assets will be distributed at death with the least amount of taxes and legal fees. Protecting your future is more than for your lifetime alone but also the lifetimes of those you know and love, your children and grandchildren, or other people or institutions you care about, especially for those who do not have children. In other words, your legacy.

Ettinger Law Firm, thirty-three years old as of this writing, was founded in 1991, after your author had been practicing as a litigation attorney for ten plus years in New York City as well as in the Hudson Valley and Capital Region of New York State.

Introduction

In the Fall of 1990, I first heard of a new concept in law, that if you set up a living trust your estate would no longer have to go through the legal process to prove your will was valid – the probate court proceeding. Having faced many legal issues, delays and soaring costs probating wills over the previous decade, I thought this new concept almost too good to be true.

Exploring the matter further, I learned that not only was the proposition true, but at the time, some of the best attorneys practicing with the living trust concept were in Florida – perhaps you can guess why.

In any event, off I went to Florida to train in the preparation, execution and use of revocable living trusts with some of the most knowledgeable and experienced attorneys in this burgeoning field of law. Upon my return, I proceeded to wrap up my litigation practice and founded Ettinger Law Firm in April 1991 dedicated exclusively to estate planning and to keeping people like you, dear reader, out of probate court.

The reason I was so excited about the living trust, and continue to be so to this day, is the concept of taking back control from the courts and government and giving it back to you and your family. After all, who doesn't want control over their affairs?

A will has to be "probated", or proved to be valid in court. When you go to court, the judge is in charge. Does the judge always act in your best interest? Does the judge ever make a mistake? And when the judge says jump, you know what the answer is. In other words, someone else is in control of your affairs.

Not only do you pay considerably for this privilege, but it can take many months and often years to complete the probate court proceeding. Meantime, houses cannot be sold, bank accounts accessed, or investment portfolios managed – at least without the judge's permission which involves additional time and resources to request. Of course, that permission may be denied as well.

With a living trust, your trustee (formerly your "executor" under the will) may act immediately upon death to sell the house, pay the bills and handle the investments – no permission required. An additional benefit is, in the event you become unable to handle your affairs later in life, your trustee may take over by simply getting a letter from your doctor showing you are legally incapacitated – in other words unable to handle your legal and financial affairs.

Essentially then, a living trust gives you back control.

Concurrently with my beginning to practice estate planning for death a new field of law was emerging, that of "elder law". The legal profession had come to realize that numerous legal issues were arising with the aging of the population and the increased life expectancies that were occurring with advances in diet, nutrition and medicine. It seemed to me that it made sense to plan for disability (elder law) at the same time as planning for death (estate planning). I called this type of planning as "Elder Law Estate Planning" and wrote a book with that same title in 2010, updated yearly since then. While it is a law book, it is written in plain English for the purpose of communicating legal subjects to the lay person. Whenever we refer to estate planning, it is simply a shortened version of what we mean to be elder law estate planning.

Introduction

The book you are about to embark on is an outgrowth of its predecessor. It reflects the additional twenty-three years of growth and knowledge of your writer in the deeper and broader meaning of "elder law estate planning".

As before, you will learn about the tools available to protect your future, (a) from guardianship proceedings on disability (2) from losing your assets to pay for long-term care costs (3) from court proceedings on death, and (4) from taxes and legal fees in the settlement of your estate.

Added to this nuts and bolts knowledge is a new section on "Financial and Tax Aspects of Estate Planning" containing invaluable information on reducing and avoiding income, estate and capital gains taxes along with other tips for rearranging your financial affairs for greater liquidity when needed.

The first of two more new sections is on "The Social Side of Estate Planning", addressing many of the social and family issues that surround this type of planning. Your writer has come to the belief, after over forty years of doing this type of work, that estate planning is primarily a social exercise and that the social work must be done prior to the legal work -- so that the legal may serve the social needs of the clients and their loved ones and not the other way around. Too many perfectly legal estate plans have had the effect of tearing a family apart for having failed to observe this key tenet.

Secondly, we have written a new section on "Health and Well-Being for Older Adults". Your writer has been publishing a column in over a dozen New York newspapers for the past three years entitled

Introduction

"Protecting Your Future" which has led to my extensive research and writing on these subjects. The sharing of some of the latest thinking on health and well-being reflects my view that the best elder law estate plan of all, by far, is not having to use it as long as possible. To this end we are looking at the many exciting new ways to avoid disability and to extend not only lifespan but the healthy years in that lifespan, or "healthspan".

I sincerely hope that you find this book interesting, enjoyable and perhaps even life-enhancing.

Michael Ettinger
October, 2023

"Set peace of mind as your highest goal, and organize your life around it."
-- Brian Tracy

ELDER LAW ESTATE PLANNING

1

What is Elder Law Estate Planning

"Elder Law Estate Planning" is a niche area of the law which combines the features of elder law and estate planning that pertain most to the needs of the middle class.

Estate planning was originally for the wealthy few. Middle class families did not consider themselves as having "estates" to plan. During the Reagan years (1980-1988), a great economic expansion occurred, raising the asset level of the middle class into the realm of estate planning. With middle class people suddenly exposed to "estate taxes", the need arose for estate planning, to reduce or eliminate those taxes. A few years later, in 1991, the American Association of Retired Persons (AARP) published "A Consumer Report on Probate" which concluded that probate was a process to be avoided, in all but the most exceptional cases. This marked the beginning of the end of traditional will planning and started the "living trust revolution". AARP recommended that families start using trusts rather than wills, to avoid probate and save their beneficiaries tens of thousands of dollars in the estate settlement process.

Since 1991, tens of millions of people have set up trusts to:

- Save time and money in settling the estate

- Avoid legal guardianship if they become disabled

- Avoid having their personal and financial matters made public

- Reduce the chance of a "will contest"

- Keep control in their family and out of the court system

At about the same time as living trust planning became popular, the field of elder law emerged to help people navigate the increased complexity of state Medicaid rules and regulations, the soaring costs of home care and nursing home stays, and the fact that people were living considerably longer.

Historically, estate planning was handled primarily by "white shoe" law firms in the deep canyons of downtown Manhattan, while elder law planning emerged out of the Department of Social Services. State employees began to take their expertise in Medicaid rules and regulations into the private sector.

To this day, these two fields continue to grow independently of each other, sometimes to the detriment of the clients whom lawyers are meant to serve. Estate planning lawyers mostly see estates averaging from hundreds of thousands to about five million dollars. However, families with estates under one million dollars often cannot afford long-term care insurance. They may now or later need a Medicaid Asset Protection Trust (MAPT) (Chapter 48) to protect their estates from being depleted in the event a nursing home is required. Since the estate planning attorney is often unfamiliar with elder law, the client never gets the MAPT they need, and the estate plan to avoid probate proves useless when the costs of long-term care ends up consuming all of the assets.

For the couple with over one million dollars in investible assets, while they may more often be able to afford long-term care insurance, sometimes either one or both of them are uninsurable due to health reasons or they have waited until age seventy or so and the premiums are too high. Perhaps what they really need is the MAPT, to protect the assets from nursing home costs, but they never get one because the estate planning lawyer is not experienced or trained in drafting these documents.

What happens when the estate planning client actually becomes disabled and needs long-term care? They, or the family, often consult with the estate planning lawyer who prepared their plan, but who may be unable to help them, due to his or her unfamiliarity with state Medicaid rules. Many families lose assets that might have been saved. Unknown to the estate planning attorney, elder law attorneys have developed numerous techniques to protect hard won assets, even when the nursing home is imminent, such as "spousal refusal" and the "gift and loan" strategy, discussed in the chapters that follow.

On the other side of the coin, what happens when the older single or couple meets with an elder law attorney instead of an estate planning attorney? These clients are usually sixty-five or over, and are looking for asset protection. The elder law attorney knows how to create a MAPT and often recommends them. However, on the estate planning side of matters, the elder law attorney may miss the need to set up two trusts for the couple to avoid the estate tax, if they are exposed to that liability. He or she may have little knowledge about estate planning for second marriages, a growing segment of the population, or using Inheritance Protection Trusts (Chapter 6) to keep the assets in the blood and protect the inheritance from children's divorces, lawsuits, and creditors.

While some of the family's needs may be met, such as asset protection, other needs are left unserved, often because the clients are unaware that these two fields of law complement and overlap one another. In other words, they may get what they want but not necessarily what they need. These oversights are often visited on the heirs.

Your writer made the conscious decision over thirty years ago to develop expertise in these two fields of law simultaneously. This has proven to be invaluable to tens of thousands of families. Clients who originally came in for estate planning services later became elder law clients, converting their revocable living trust estate plans into MAPT's as they got older or, through the use of Medicaid planning services, ended up protecting their assets when the need for long-term care actually arose.

Looking back on our experiences in over thirty thousand cases at Ettinger Law Firm, we conclude that we have assisted in the creation of a new niche legal field, "Elder Law Estate Planning".

We define this area of law as:

- Getting your assets to your heirs, when you want and the way you want, with the least amount of taxes and legal fees possible

- Keeping those assets in the blood for your grandchildren and, in the meantime, protecting those assets from your children's divorces, lawsuits, and creditors

- Protecting your assets from the costs of long-term care and qualifying you for government benefits available to pay for that care

While estate planning involves tools for well-to-do families, with acronyms like GRITS, GRATS, and GRUTS, and where elder law serves the diverse needs of our growing senior population, including the less fortunate, through Medicaid, Medicare and Social Security, "Elder Law Estate Planning" addresses the concerns of the vast majority in the middle. It is for those people that we have written this book.

2

Pitfalls of Will Planning

So many clients are advised that they need a will. In fact, will planning is becoming obsolete for persons over sixty for many reasons.

Instead of actually solving problems, wills often create them. First, they must be proven to be valid in a court proceeding, the infamous probate. Court proceedings may be expensive, time-consuming and things often go wrong. Also, when the client dies, that will is often out-of-date, having been created decades before. The executors may be the wrong persons, the beneficiaries or their percentages may be wrong or other changes in the family have not been taken into account.

Notice of the court proceeding must be given to certain relatives who may be difficult or impossible to locate. Complications arise with relatives in foreign countries who may need to go to the American Consulate for notarization or "consularization" of legal documents. If there is a disabled child, the court will appoint a lawyer to represent that heir's interests, including preparing a report to the court, and your estate must pay that attorney's fees.

Proof problems with the will may lead to delays preventing needed funds from getting to surviving spouses or children. It is fairly common for real estate to be tied up, while the probate process drags on, causing potential buyers to be lost. In some cases, stock cannot be sold even though it may be falling in value rapidly. Bills can remain unpaid for lengthy periods as bank accounts are unavailable. Law firms routinely find they must commence probate proceedings as a courtesy for families who cannot afford the legal fees to get the matter started. The cost of court proceedings today may be expected to be in the five figure range.

Two other pitfalls of will planning bear mentioning. First, since the will is filed in court, it becomes a public record. Anyone may go to the courthouse and order a copy of your will to see what you had and who you left it to. Secondly, since notice must be given to the heirs you may have left out, or left less than they may feel they are entitled to, you run the risk of a will contest if your estate is distributed in anything but equal shares.

When you are in probate court, who is in charge? The judge, not you or your lawyer. Don't suppose that the judge will always act in your best interests, as the court may have other interests to consider.

Always better to stay out of court if you can. By using a living trust, instead of a will, you may avoid probate court proceedings and keep control, or at least control rests with those you have chosen, if you die or become disabled. The expenses are sufficiently less without court proceedings that clients often save tens of thousands of dollars in estate settlement costs.

The other problem with a will? It only takes effect when you die. Today, about half of all people eventually become disabled. Since the will does not provide for disability, you risk guardianship proceedings. These proceedings occur later in life when someone becomes unable to handle their affairs and does not have an adequate plan set up for disability. In a guardianship, the court will appoint someone to handle your affairs. Not only may it not be the person you would have chosen, it may not even be someone you know. Trusts, which take effect while you are living, are considered a highly effective tool to avoid guardianship proceedings so that the person or persons you choose will be in charge. This way, you may be certain that your best interests will be looked after.

In short, when someone tells you that you need a will, think again. It may be a trust that you need instead.

"During my life, and now by my will and codicils, I have given considerable sums of money to promote public and humanitarian causes which have had my deliberate and sympathetic interest. If any of my children think excessive such gifts of mine outside of the family, I ask them to remember not only the merit of the causes and the corresponding usefulness of the gifts but also the dominating ideals of my life.

They should never forget the dangers which unfortunately attend the inheritance of large fortunes, even though the money come from the painstaking affections of a father. I beg of them to remember that such danger lies not only in the obvious temptation to enervating luxury, but in the inducement...to withdraw from the wholesome duty of vigorous, serious, useful work. In my opinion a life not largely dedicated to such work cannot be happy and honorable. And to such it is my earnest hope – and will be to my death – that my children shall, so far as their strength permits, be steadfastly devoted."

Joseph Pulitzer, Will, in James Wyman Barrett,
Joseph Pulitzer and His World **295-96 (1941)**

3

The Five Steps to an Elder Law Estate Plan

Overview

Practicing elder law estate planning is one of the most enjoyable and professionally rewarding careers an attorney may choose. Imagine a practice area where your clients respect your knowledge and treat you with kindness and courtesy. They pay your fees in a timely fashion and tell their friends how much they have enjoyed working with you and your firm. At the same time, you are rarely facing the pressure of a deadline, much less an adversarial attorney on the other side of a matter trying to beat you. In most instances, you are acting in the capacity of a counselor at law (trusted advisor) rather than an attorney at law (professional representative).

We spend our days meeting with clients, discussing their lives and their families and addressing their fears and concerns. Through our knowledge, training, experience and imagination, we craft solutions, occasionally elegant ones, to the age old problem of passing assets from one generation to another as quickly and painlessly as possible.

At the same time, we also seek to protect those assets from being depleted by taxes, legal fees and long-term care costs to the extent the law allows.

The end result of this process is a client who feels safe and secure in the knowledge that, in the event of death or disability, they have all their bases covered. Having achieved peace of mind that their future is well planned and in good hands, they can get on with the business of enjoying their lives. For the attorney, a happy and satisfied client has been added to the practice and another potentially lifelong and mutually rewarding relationship has begun. Let's look at the strategies and techniques we use to achieve this enviable state of affairs.

Major Issues Facing Senior Clients Today

One of the ways that we help clients is in setting up a comprehensive plan so they may avoid court proceedings upon death or in the event of disability. Trusts are used in place of wills for older persons since they do not require court proceedings to settle the estate. Trusts also avoid the foreign probate proceeding required for property owned in another state, known as ancillary probate. This saves the family time in settling the estate as well as the high costs of legal proceedings. In addition, since revocable living trusts, unlike wills, take effect during the grantor's lifetime, the client may stipulate which persons take over in the event of their disability. Planning ahead helps maintain control in the family or with trusted advisors and avoids a situation that may not be in the client's best interest. For example, in the event of a disability where no plan has been put in place, an application to the court may be required in order to have a legal guardian appointed for the disabled person. This may not be the person the client would have chosen. In such a case, assets may not be transferred to protect them from being spent down for long-term care costs without court permission, which may or may not be granted.

Another area in which we assist the client is in saving state estate taxes for married couples by using the two-trust technique. Assets are divided as evenly as practicable between each of the spouse's trusts. While the surviving spouse has the use and enjoyment of the deceased spouse's trust, the assets of that trust bypass the estate of the surviving spouse and go directly to the named beneficiaries when the second spouse dies. The two trusts are known as "disclaimer trusts", discussed in Chapter 25. Hundreds of thousands of dollars, or more, in potential estate taxes may be saved, depending on the size of the estate. Furthermore, the revocable living trust avoids the two probates that would occur were the clients to use wills, as the couple's estate must be settled after the death of each spouse in order to save estate taxes.

We also help to protect assets from being depleted due to long-term care costs. Medicaid Asset Protection Trusts (MAPT's), discussed in Chapter 48, may be established, subject to a five-year look-back period for facility care or a new two and a half year look-back for home care, to protect the client's home and other assets from having to be spent down due to the high cost of long-term care. Elder law attorneys use Medicaid asset and transfer rules to protect assets in the event a client requires long-term care but has done no pre-planning. Through the use of Medicaid annuities, the "gift and loan" strategy, spousal refusal, and Caregiver Agreements, significant assets may be protected despite the look-back periods, even when the client may be on the nursing home doorstep. These techniques are discussed in "Medicaid Planning Strategies" at page 105.

The Five Steps to an Elder Law Estate Plan

Step One: Understanding the Family Dynamics

The first step in an elder law estate planning matter is to gain an understanding of the client's family dynamics. If there are children, which is usually the case, we need to determine whether or not they are married. Is it a first or second marriage? Do they have any children from a previous marriage or do their spouses? What kind of work do they do, and where do they live? Do they get along with each other and with the parent clients? We are looking to determine which family members do not get along with which others and what the reasons may be. This goes a long way toward helping us decide who should make medical decisions and who should handle legal and financial affairs. Should it be one of them or more than one? Should they be able to act separately or only together? How should the estate be divided? Is the client himself in a second marriage? Which children, if any, are his, hers, or theirs? Sometimes all three instances may occur in the same couple. Here, further exploration of the family functioning will

Elder Law Estate Planning

be needed as the potential for hurt feelings, conflicts of interest, and misunderstandings multiplies. In addition, great care must be taken to develop a plan for management, control, and distribution of the estate that will not only be fair to the children from a previous marriage but will be seen to be fair as well. At times, the assistance of the professional advisor in acting as trustee may be invaluable in helping to keep the peace between family members. Finally, this step will also flesh out whether there are any dependents with special needs and which family members and assets might be best suited to provide for any such children.

Step Two: Reviewing Existing Estate Planning Documents

The second step in an elder law estate planning matter is to review any prior estate planning documents the client may have, such as a will, trust, power of attorney, health care proxy and living will, to determine whether they are legally sufficient and reflect the client's current wishes or whether they are outdated. Some basic elder law estate planning questions are also addressed at this time such as:

a. Is the client a US citizen? This may impinge on the client's ability to save estate taxes.

b. Is the client expecting to receive an inheritance? This knowledge helps in preparing a plan that will address not only the assets that the client has now but what they may have in the future.

c. Does the client have long-term care insurance? If so, the attorney will want to review the policy and determine whether it provides an adequate benefit considering the client's other assets and income, whether it takes inflation into account, and whether it is upgradable. This will allow the practitioner to decide whether other asset protection strategies may be needed now or later.

d. Does the client need financial planning? Many clients that come into the attorney's office have never had professional financial advice or are dissatisfied with their current advisors. They may need help understanding the assets they have or with organizing and consolidating them for ease of administration. They may also be concerned with not having enough income to last for the rest of their lives. The elder law estate planning attorney will typically know a number of capable financial planners who are experienced with the needs and wishes of the senior client, including (1) secure investments with protection of principal, and (2) assets that tend to maximize income.

Step Three: Reviewing the Client's Assets

The third step is to obtain a complete list of the client's assets, including how they are titled, their value, whether they are qualified investments, such as IRA's and 401(k)'s and, if they have beneficiary designations, who those beneficiaries are. Armed with this information, the counsellor is in a position to determine whether the estate will be subject to estate taxes, both state and federal, and may begin to formulate a strategy to reduce or eliminate those taxes to the extent the law allows. This will often lead to shifting assets between spouses and their trusts, changing beneficiary designations, and, with discretion, sometimes trying to determine which spouse might pass away first so as to effect the greatest possible tax savings. Ideally, the attorney should have the client fill out a confidential financial questionnaire prior to the initial consultation.

Step Four: Developing the Elder Law Estate Plan

The fourth step is to determine, with input from the client, who should make medical decisions for the client if they are unable to, i.e. the health care proxy, and who should be appointed to handle legal and financial affairs, i.e. the power of attorney, in the event of the client's incapacity. Next, we will consider what type of trust, if any, should be used, or whether a simple will would suffice, who should be the trustees (for a trust) or executors (for a will), and what the plan of distribution should be. In order to avoid a conflict, the trustees who are chosen to act in lieu of the grantor (creator) should be the same persons named on the power of attorney. At this point, great care should also be taken to ensure that the feelings of the heirs will not be hurt. Good estate planning looks at the client's estate from the heirs' point of view as well as the client's. For example, if there are three children, it may be preferable that one be named as trustee or executor, as three are usually too cumbersome and if the client chooses only two, then they are leaving one out. If there are four or five children, we prefer to see two trustees or executors chosen. This way, the pressure will be reduced on just the one having to answer to all the others. More importantly, the others will feel more secure with two siblings jointly looking after their interests.

Not all estates need to be distributed equally. An old adage in estate planning goes like this "There's nothing so unequal as the equal treatment of unequals".

If the distribution is to be unequal, it may need to be discussed with the affected children ahead of time to forestall any ill will or even litigation after the parents have died. By considering the relative ages of the children, where they live, and their relationships amongst each other and with their parents, the advisor will generally find a way to craft a plan that accommodates the needs and desires of all parties concerned. Some of the techniques we find useful in this context are to offer a delayed distribution, such as twenty percent upon the death of the grantor, one-half of the remaining balance after five years, and the remainder after ten years. These same percentages may also be used at stated ages, such as thirty, thirty-five, and forty. Also, when leaving percentages of the estate, unless it is simply to the children in equal shares, it is often useful to determine the monetary value of those percentages in the client's current estate. This will allow the client to see whether the amount is truly what they wish to bequeath. Percentage bequests to charities should be avoided so that the family may avoid the possibility of having to account to the charity for the expenses of administering the estate.

In terms of the type of trust, we are generally looking at several options for most clients. For couples, it is important to determine whether there should be one trust or two. In order to avoid or reduce estate taxes, there should be two trusts for spouses whose estates exceed or may at a later date exceed the state and/or federal estate tax threshold. Should the trust be revocable or irrevocable? The latter is important for protecting assets from long-term care expenses subject to the five-year look-back period for facility care and the new two and a half year look-back for home care. Primary features of the irrevocable Medicaid Asset Protection Trust (MAPT) are that neither the grantor nor the grantor's spouse may be the trustee and that these trusts are "income-only" trusts. Most people choose one or more of their adult children to act as trustees of the MAPT. Since principal is not available to the grantor, the client will not want to put all of their assets into such a trust. Assets that should be left out are IRA's, 401(k)'s, 403(b)'s, etc. The principal of these qualified assets are exempt from Medicaid and should not be placed into a trust, as this would create a taxable event requiring income taxes to be paid on all of the qualified money. If the institutionalized client has a spouse in the community, up to $150,000 may also be exempted. Notwithstanding that the home, at least up to about $1,000,000 in equity, is exempt if the community spouse is living there, it is generally a good idea to protect the home now rather than to wait until the first spouse has passed, due to the look-back periods. It should be noted that the look-back means that from the time assets are transferred to the MAPT, it takes five years before they are exempt, or protected from being required to be spent down on the ill person's care in a nursing facility before they qualify for Medicaid benefits. What if the client does not make the five years? Imagine that the client must go into the nursing home four years after the trust has been established. In such a case, by privately paying the nursing facility for the one year remaining, the family will be eligible for Medicaid after just the remaining year of the five-year penalty period has expired.

Although the MAPT is termed irrevocable, the home may still be sold or other trust assets traded. This does not restart the lookback. The trust itself, through the actions of the trustees, may sell the house and purchase a condominium in the name of the trust so that the asset is still protected. The trust may sell one stock and buy another. For those clients who may wish to continue trading on their own, the adult child trustee may sign a third party authorization with the brokerage firm authorizing the parent to continue trading on the account. Sometimes this is simply done online with the parent using the PIN on the account. The trust continues to pay all income (i.e., interest and dividends) to the parent grantor. As such, the irrevocable trust payments should not affect the client's lifestyle when added to any pensions, social security, and IRA or other qualified distributions the client continues receiving from outside the trust. Homeowners insurance should be modified to add the trustees, who are now on the deed, as additional insureds. MAPT's are discussed in more detail following.

If there is a special needs child, consideration will be given to creating a Special Needs Trust (Chapter 9), which will pay over and above what the child may be receiving in government benefits, especially social security income and Medicaid, so that the inheritance will not disqualify them from those benefits.

With the size of estates having grown today to where middle class families are leaving substantial bequests to their children (depending, of course, on how many children they have), the trend is toward establishing trusts for the children to keep the inheritance in the bloodline. Variously termed Inheritance Protection Trusts, Heritage Trusts, or Dynasty Trusts, these trusts may contain additional features, such as protecting the inheritance from a child's divorce, lawsuits and creditors during their lifetimes, and estate taxes when they die. The primary feature of all of these trusts for the heirs, however, is to provide that when the child dies, in most cases many years after the parent, the hard-earned assets of the family will not pass to an in-law who may get remarried and eventually share those assets with a stranger, but rather to the grantor's grandchildren. On the other hand, if the client wishes to favor the son-in-law or daughter-in-law, they may choose to provide that the trust, or a portion of it, continue as an "income only" trust for their adult child's surviving spouse for their lifetime, and only thereafter to the grantor's grandchildren.

Other key areas for discussion in developing the elder law estate plan are second marriage planning, planning for those without children, protecting assets for spendthrift children, and planning for same-sex couples, topics discussed in more detail in later chapters.

Step Five: Executing and Maintaining the Plan

At the meeting to execute the elder law estate plan, the documents are reviewed with the client, explanations are given and questions are answered. Many practitioners favor sending the documents ahead of time for their clients' review. While there are advantages to this practice, we have found the clients are often overwhelmed by the legal documents and prefer to limit the practice to those instances where it is specifically requested.

After execution, including signing new deeds transferring real property into the trust, the client is advised how to transfer title of their investments and bank accounts to the trust. Similarly, beneficiary designations on annuities, life insurance policies and sometimes on IRA's and other qualified plans are often changed to the client's trust or to the children's Inheritance Protection Trusts.

In the event there is more than one trust being executed, which assets are left to which trust, and why, are explained to the client as part of the process of funding the trusts.

Finally, the elder law estate plan is reviewed every three years for changes in the law as well as changes in the lives of the clients and their families. Inherent in the plan is the ability of the "hybrid" elder law estate planning firm to address Medicaid asset protection issues, either by planning ahead due to advancing years or, in the event of an "immediate need", when a crisis arises and the family has failed to take action in advance. Medicaid planning strategies, key tools in the elder law estate planning attorney's toolbox, are also discussed in greater detail following.

At our firm, we believe not only reviewing the plan every three years, but also in building the attorney-client relationship. To that end, we send our clients a weekly article on some interesting or important elder law and estate planning topic. This way, the elder law estate plan is far more likely to address their situation when they may need to use it in the future. Indeed, by providing ongoing information and reviewing the client's matter tri-annually, the elder law estate plan is designed to work when the client needs it, not when they wrote it, perhaps decades earlier.

4

The Two Biggest Mistakes in Planning

1. Failure to address all of the issues.

A comprehensive review of the client's situation should address planning for disability as well as for death, including minimizing or avoiding estate taxes and legal fees and proceedings. A plan should be in place to protect assets from long-term care costs. Like a chess player, counsel should look ahead two or three moves in order to determine what may happen in the future. For example, attorneys will too often place a majority of the assets in the wife's name or in her trust in light of the husband having significant IRA or any qualified assets in his account. However, since the husband is often older and has a shorter life expectancy, this may result in the IRA type assets rolling over to the wife, all of the couple's assets ending up in the wife's estate, and no estate tax savings effected.

Another example would be where the client's children are in a second marriage but have children (the client's grandchildren) from a previous marriage. Unless planning is done with Inheritance Protection Trusts (Chapter 6) for the client's children, a situation may occur one day where the client's child predeceases their second spouse, all assets pass to the second spouse, and the client's grandchildren, from a son or daughter's prior marriage, are denied any benefit from the grantor's estate.

2. Failure to Regularly Review the Elder Law Estate Plan

At a minimum, each client's estate plan should be reviewed every three years to determine whether changes in the client's personal life, such as their health, assets, or family history (births, deaths, marriages, divorces, etc.) impact the plan. It is unrealistic to expect a plan established today to be effective ten, twenty, thirty, or more years in the future. Over time, clients will want to change their back-up trustees or plan of distribution. They may wish to add Inheritance Protection Trusts for their children. They might, after a number of years, wish to change from a revocable trust to a MAPT because they were unable or unwilling to obtain long-term care insurance. The client will benefit from having a plan better suited to their current needs at any given time.

Despite the knowledge and earnestness of some of the best practitioners in the land, clients sometimes do not act on the advice given. Experienced attorneys know not to take it personally when clients choose to ignore their advice or perhaps choose other counsel. People don't always do what they need to, they do what they want to do. A ninety-three year old client once told us that she "wanted to think about it" so far as planning her affairs. Experience tells us that this client is not ready to plan at the present time, despite her advanced years, and we must respect that choice. On the other hand, we recall a client coming in to see us eleven years after their initial consultation stating that they were now ready to proceed. We prepared their elder law estate plan.

5

Components of an Elder Law Estate Plan

For most clients, an Elder Law Estate Plan consists of the following documents and features:

1. A Revocable Living Trust (RLT) or an Irrevocable Medicaid Asset Protection Trust (MAPT)

Generally the client will have one of these trusts or the other, not both. The MAPT is used where protection of assets is required in the absence of long-term care insurance. For married couples with estates over the estate tax exemption, state and/or Federal, two trusts may be required, one for each spouse, to create two estates thereby doubling the exemption from estate taxes. Where clients wish to protect the inheritance from children's divorces, lawsuits and creditors, and keep the inheritance in the bloodline so it passes to grandchildren instead of to in-laws or strangers, Inheritance Protection Trusts may be added as an option to either the Revocable Living Trust (RLT) or the MAPT. These Inheritance Protection Trusts are "stand-by trusts". They remain empty until the parent dies or, if there is a spouse, until the surviving spouse dies, and then the parents' trust or trusts pay out to the children's Inheritance Protection Trusts.

2. Pour-Over Will

A new will which cancels your old will and provides that in case you may have left anything outside of your trust, the assets should be "poured into" your trust after you are gone, since your wishes are provided in the trust. Care should be taken to ensure that any assets left outside the trust are either joint with someone else or have a designated beneficiary. The use of the pour-over will is to be avoided, if possible, since it must be probated. It is there "just in case".

Examples of where a pour-over will might be used are (a) the client dies while waiting for an inheritance that is tied up in a probate proceeding, or (b) the client dies in a car accident and the estate comes into money damages, for wrongful death.

3. Power of Attorney

Allows the person or persons you choose to handle your legal and financial affairs should you be unable to for any reason. There are distinct advantages to having an elder law estate planning attorney draft the power of attorney. Since we deal with disability on a daily basis, we are more aware of the essential powers that may be needed should a client become disabled. Some of the common powers that have been found useful to add to standard form powers are:

   a. To change beneficiaries on IRA's, annuities and insurance policies

   b. To create, fund or modify a trust

   c. To make gifts in unlimited amounts

These additional powers may make the difference between the client qualifying for Medicaid benefits one day or losing some or all of their assets to pay for their care. Powers of Attorney are discussed in Chapter 7.

4. Health Care Proxy/Living Will

The proxy is the person who you wish to make medical decisions for you if you are unable to decide for yourself. The living will authorizes termination of life support systems, such as feeding tubes and ventilators, when your proxy determines that is best.

The general standard here is to withdraw life sustaining measures when the agent determines that the patient no longer has any meaningful existence and there is no hope of recovery. Nevertheless, it is important to note that the agent is carrying out the patient's express wishes, not those of the agent themselves. Health care decision-making is further discussed in Chapter 8.

5. Funeral and Burial Instructions

In your own handwriting you may provide:

    a. Type of funeral service

    b. Type of burial

    c. Whether funeral has been prepaid

    d. Who will be in charge of the arrangements

    e. What organs and tissues you may wish to donate

6. Final Instructions to Your Family

A form to fill out giving your family basic information they will need to settle your estate including:

    a. Date and place of any marriage

    b. Subscriptions that need to be cancelled

    c. Your computer user names and passwords

    d. Family, friends, businesses and professional advisors who should be contacted in the event of death

    e. Any information you would like included in your obituary

f. Safe deposit box instructions and key

g. Checklist of what needs to be done by those settling your affairs, such as contacting Social Security and the Post Office

7. Deeds

New deeds should be prepared transferring your real property from your name into the name of your trust. This is important for out-of-state property as well to avoid a second probate in the other jurisdiction.

8. Memorandum of Personal Effects

Modern practice is to leave a handwritten list of which valuables go to which of the heirs and to request that the trustee honor the terms of the memorandum for those special items. This way, the client does not need to see the attorney to change their estate plan for personal effects. If they change their mind as to these personal items, they may simply tear up the old memorandum and write a new one.

9. Instructions for Transferring Assets to Your Trust

Although this is explained in person at the time the trust is executed, a written set of instructions will accompany the documents as well. Many law firms, including ours, will undertake to assist you in this process. However, many clients are able to do this for themselves.

10. Monitoring and Maintaining the Plan

At a minimum, a program should be in place to review the plan at least once every three years for changes in the law as well as in the client's assets, their health or in their personal lives and those of their heirs, such as births, death, marriages and divorces. This way, in the event of death or disability, which may occur many years later, the plan is always current. A law firm newsletter is also recommended to keep the client abreast of any law changes that may affect their plan on an ongoing basis.

6

Inheritance Protection Trusts (IPT)

With the size of estates having grown today to where middle class families are leaving substantial bequests to their children (depending, of course, on how many children they have), the trend is toward establishing trusts for the children to keep the inheritance in the bloodline. In the case of your children, there are a number of benefits to leaving assets to them in a trust. These are: (1) the assets will be protected from claims by their spouse in the event of divorce (2) the assets may be protected from their creditors in the event of a lawsuit or other financial hardship, and (3) on your child's death, the unused assets will go to your blood relatives (usually grandchildren) instead of to in-laws or others.

We call this "multi-generational planning". Whereas with a will your estate plan usually dies when you do, with an Inheritance Protection Trust your wishes will go on for thirty, forty or even fifty or more years after you are gone, i.e., for two generations instead of just one.

These trusts provide that, during your children's lifetimes, they have complete access to the income and the principal of their Inheritance Protection Trusts – so that you're not giving them a "gift with strings attached" or "ruling from the grave". The Inheritance Protection Trust is also a "sprinkling" or "spray" trust, meaning the assets may be used by your son or daughter not only for themselves, but also for your grandchildren, in equal or unequal shares. When your child dies, the Inheritance Protection Trust which you have established directs that the remaining trust assets, which may have grown considerably, go to your grandchildren. If the grandchildren are under age thirty-five, we recommend that the funds be held in trust for them until such age, with the trustee (usually an aunt or uncle) using so much of the assets as may be needed for their health, education, maintenance and support. If one of your children dies without leaving children of their own, then the trust funds go to their surviving brothers and sisters.

Keep in mind that, without an Inheritance Protection Trust, if your son or daughter dies, the entire inheritance you have left may go to a son-in-law or daughter-in-law who may later get remarried and share your hard earned assets with a complete stranger. Nevertheless, some clients would not want to completely leave out their son-in-law or daughter-in-law. In such cases, the Inheritance Protection Trust, or a portion of it, such as one-half, may be set up to continue for your in-law's lifetime, providing them with the "income only" so that if they get remarried or end up in a nursing home, the assets are still protected. On their death the remaining trust principal will then go to your grandchildren or whomever else you designate.

7

Powers of Attorney

What happens if you have an accident or an illness whereby you are unable to handle your legal and financial affairs? Many people incorrectly believe their spouse is legally able to handle their affairs. Similarly, a parent has no legal authority to handle the affairs of a child, once the child attains the age of majority – eighteen years.

Without a power of attorney, you would have to apply to a court to be named a legal guardian. These proceedings are expensive, time-consuming and fraught with peril. The judge has no obligation to name the spouse or parent as legal guardian and may appoint a stranger. For example, the judge may feel that the spouse or parent has a conflict in that they are the beneficiary of the incapacitated person's assets, or the judge may decide that someone else has more knowledge and experience in handling such matters.

Who should you choose as your "agent"? In our experience, the vast majority of powers of attorney name the spouse first and one or more of the children second. While on its face this seems reasonable, experience has shown it may not be a good idea. We often need to use the power of attorney when the client is quite elderly and infirm. Often, so is the spouse at that time. Son or daughter wants to step in and help out with bill paying, etc. only to find they are unable to use the power of attorney for dad unless they can prove that mom can't.

How do you prove she can't? First you have to get the doctor to write a letter that mom is unable to handle her legal and financial affairs. Will the doctor write the letter? Will the letter be clear and unequivocal? Will each of the third parties you have to deal with accept the letter? These are not easy hurdles to overcome.

We believe there is a better way. We simply say either mom, or son, or daughter may act as agent. The problem is eliminated. You are protected from son or daughter misusing the power of attorney by the fact that they do not have the document – you keep it in your possession and make it available if and when they need to use it.

Despite the fact that every adult should have a power of attorney, not all powers of attorney are created equal. The standard form, used by many attorneys, is what we term "over the counter medicine". Instead, we choose to use what we call the "prescription strength" elder law power of attorney.

It works just like medicine. What happens when you only have over the counter medicine but you need prescription strength?

You know what happens – it doesn't work, it's not strong enough. For example, the standard form allows the agent to make gifts up to $5,000 per year. The elder law power of attorney has no such limitation, allowing the agent to gift any amount. Let's say a client is going into a nursing home or needs care at home. We often save the family hundreds of thousands of dollars using the elder law power of attorney to gift out to the children those amounts that will help qualify the client for Medicaid benefits. Generally, even on the nursing home doorstep, we can save about half of a parent's assets by gifting.

Now, if the client only has the standard power of attorney, they can only gift five thousand dollars a year. When it comes to Medicaid, it's move it or lose it! Almost all of mom's money will have to be used for her care.

Let's say mom has $500,000 in assets and needs nursing facility care. We use the elder law power of attorney to gift $250,000 to the children (tax-free). So long as we use the remaining $250,000 to pay for mom's care, the family gets to keep the $250,000 gift. Other valuable powers added to the elder law power of attorney are (1) powers to create or modify trusts (2) powers to change beneficiaries on IRA's, annuities and insurance policies, and (3) powers to refuse any inheritances left to the disabled person.

For clients age sixty and older, choosing an elder law attorney often makes the difference between losing and keeping your home and life savings to pay for long-term care.

8

Health Care Decision-Making

For health care decision-making, when a doctor determines you are unable to make medical decisions for yourself, New York has the Health Care Proxy. The proxy, or agent, may make any medical decision for you except one – they cannot withdraw life sustaining measures, such as feeding tubes or a ventilator, unless they can prove this is what you actually wanted.

There are two ways to show that, in situations where there is no reasonable expectation of recovery from extreme disability, and there is no meaningful existence, you do not wish to be kept alive by artificial means. First, you may state in your health care proxy form that you have discussed your wishes regarding artificial life support with your proxy and they know what your wishes are or, secondly, you may execute a 'living will' which is essentially a statement that you do not wish to be kept alive in the circumstances discussed above.

The primary consideration in choosing an agent is who would be best suited to make these end-of-life decisions. Most people choose a spouse first and one of their children second. Nevertheless, there is no requirement that it be a family member. You may choose whoever you wish. We are often asked if the client can choose two or more of their children to act jointly. For good reason, the Public Health Law disallows this — if the joint agents didn't agree, how would the doctor know what to do?

A few years ago, a client came into our office and explained that his mother had been on a feeding tube for two years. He went on to say that she could not open her eyes, speak or get out of bed. Incredulous, we asked if she had signed a Living Will. He said yes she had. We then inquired what happened when he went to visit her. He stated that when he put his hand in hers, she was able to squeeze his finger. Our conclusion? She may have chosen the wrong person as her health care proxy. Choosing someone who is strong enough to carry out your wishes is essential.

As opposed to the health care proxy, Medical Orders for Life-Sustaining Treatment (MOLST) forms are medical directives signed by a doctor and used to convey a patient's wishes regarding life-sustaining treatment. The purpose is to improve the quality of care that seriously ill people receive at the end of life.

A survey by BlueCross revealed only 42% of those surveyed had chosen a health care proxy, so most people are without an advance directive for medical decisions. The Family Health Care Decisions Act allows a close family member or friend to make health care decisions for incapacitated loved ones who do not have a health care agent or didn't previously make such decisions.

The Family Health Care Decisions Act designates, in order of priority, who can act as a surrogate for the adult incapacitated person. The first surrogate is the spouse or domestic partner. The list then includes adult child, parent, sibling, and last, a close friend. If the court has appointed a legal guardian, that person takes priority.

Decisions are based on the patient's wishes or the patient's best interests if the patient's wishes are unknown. The MOLST form and The Family Health Care Decisions Act are advancements in honoring each person's end of life desires regarding medical treatment.

However, it can't be stressed enough - the best way to honor one's desires regarding end of life medical treatment is to complete a Health Care Proxy and Living Will in advance.

9

Special Needs Trusts (SNT)

Parents or grandparents of a special needs child should leave assets in a Special Needs Trust, to avoid the child being disqualified from receiving government benefits, such as SSI and Medicaid. The reasoning behind these Special Needs Trusts is simple — prior to the protection now afforded by these trusts, parents would simply disinherit their special needs children rather than see them lose their benefits. Since the state wasn't getting the inheritance monies anyway, why not allow it to go to the child for his or her extra needs, above and beyond what the state supplies, such as:

- Clothing
- Essential dietary needs
- Education
- Hobbies, sports, exercise

- Tickets for events
- Health care costs and medical procedures
- Vocational rehabilitation
- Household goods (appliances, furniture, computer, television)
- Personal care products
- Personal services (lawn mowing, housecleaning, baby-sitting, etc.)
- Music
- Real property
- Automobile (including gas and insurance)
- Transportation (buses, cabs, trains, domestic airfare)
- Vacations
- Burial costs

These trusts, however, offer traps for the unwary. Since payments to the child will generally reduce their SSI payments dollar for dollar, trustees of such trusts should be advised to make payments directly to the providers of goods and services. Preserving SSI benefits is crucial since eligibility for SSI determines eligibility for Medicaid.

In other words, if SSI is lost the recipient also loses their Medicaid benefits. In addition, any benefits previously paid by Medicaid may be recovered. As such, one also has to be mindful of bequests from well-meaning grandparents. Similarly, if a sibling dies without a will, a share of their estate would go to the special needs brother or sister by law.

Distributions from the trust to the beneficiary should be "in kind" rather than in cash. For example, the trust may own items such as furniture and allow the beneficiary child the use of them. In addition, the Special Needs Trust must be carefully drafted so that it only allows payments for any benefits over and above what the government provides, not only now but also in the future. The child may not control or have direct access to any portion of the trust.

There are two types of Special Needs Trusts. First party and third party. The first party trust is set up by a parent, grandparent, legal guardian or court using the child's own money, either through earnings, an inheritance that was left directly to them or, perhaps, a personal injury award. Recent changes in the law allow the special needs child to establish their own first party Special Needs Trust if they are legally competent to engage in contractual matters. These first party trusts require a "payback" provision, meaning that on the death of the child beneficiary, the trust must pay back the state for any government benefits received. In other words, the state is saying that, we will let you use this money for your special needs, but whatever was not needed should go back towards your basic care. These trusts require annual reporting and accounting to the state and are limited to children under age sixty-five.

A third party trust is usually set up by a parent or grandparent, using their own money. Here, no "payback" provision is required because it was not the child's own money that funded the trust and the parent or grandparent had no obligation to leave any assets to the child. Indeed, requiring a payback provision would discourage many parents from setting up a Special Needs Trust at all. Generally, on the death of the child beneficiary, the balance of the trust is paid out to the special needs child's children first, if any, otherwise to the surviving siblings, then nieces and nephews, etc.

A major issue for parents today is the increased life expectancy of their special needs child. With major advances in medical care, many such children, who would have in earlier days predeceased their parents, are now surviving them. In order to solve this problem, parents often leave a disproportionate share of the estate to the special needs child. This can engender hard feelings in siblings who, although agreeable to such an arrangement initially, may find themselves in need of funds later on and resentful of the uneven distribution in favor of the special needs child. The surviving siblings are often the only support network available for the special needs child so it is all the more important to keep peace and harmony in the family.

Often, an analysis with the elder law estate planning attorney will reveal that the assets from an equal division of the estate will, in fact, be sufficient to provide for the special needs child. If such is not the case, "second-to-die", or "survivorship life", insurance may be purchased to provide for any additional funds needed. These policies are written over both parent's lives. Since the insurance company only has to pay when the second parent dies, the premiums are significantly lower than on a single life policy. Consideration should also be given to having the policy owned by an Irrevocable Life Insurance Trust, for tax purposes.

Finally, in order to assist those who may have to care for the special needs child after the parent is gone, a "Letter of Intent" is often used. Here, the parent advises about any daily medical needs, their daily routines, their likes and dislikes, etc. Samples of the "Letter of Intent" for a special needs child are available on the internet.

10

Trusts for Minor Grandchildren

Generally, parents leave their assets to the children thinking that the children will then take care of their children. Occasionally, parents want to bypass the children, either wholly or partially, and leave an inheritance directly to the grandchildren.

Inheritances to minors come in different varieties, such as bequests in wills and as beneficiaries or contingent beneficiaries on IRA's, investment accounts, life insurance policies and annuities.

Although well-intentioned, inheritances to minors, without a trust, must go through a court proceeding on death. Minors, those under 18, cannot hold property in their names. In the proceeding, the judge appoints a legal guardian to protect the minor's interest until age eighteen, at which time the beneficiary receives the asset.

The expenses of the legal guardian will be paid out of the minor's bequest. Generally, the legal guardian will use the funds for the child's health, education, maintenance and support having regard to any other assets or resources of the minor known to the guardian. Again, ready or not, the legal guardian must turn over the assets to the minor at age eighteen, a tender age in today's world.

A better plan would be to leave assets to a minor beneficiary by creating a trust. You leave directions for the use of the funds, distribution at a stated age, such as thirty years old and, in the meantime, the trustee, a person you choose instead of a legal guardian chosen by the court, uses the money for the purposes enumerated above, either by giving money directly to the beneficiary or by paying bills on their behalf.

Trusts avoid probate court proceedings entirely for the trust assets. You either put assets into the trust while you are living or, alternatively, you may name the minor's trust as death beneficiary on bank accounts, investment accounts, IRA's or the retirement plans, annuities and life insurance policies.

The intention to benefit minor beneficiaries must be attended to with thoughtful planning to avoid having the good deed punished.

11

Second Marriage Planning

In second marriage planning, a co-trustee is sometimes recommended on the death of the first spouse. While both spouses are living and competent they run their trust or trusts together. But when one spouse dies, what prevents the other spouse from diverting all of the assets to their own children? Nothing at all, if they alone are in charge. While most people are honorable, and many are certain their spouse would never do such a thing, strange things often happen later in life. A spouse may become forgetful, delusional or senile or may be influenced by other parties. Not only that, but the children of the deceased spouse tend to feel very insecure when they find out their stepparent is in charge of all of the couple's assets.

If you choose one of the deceased spouse's children to act as co-trustee with the surviving spouse there is a conflict that exists whereby the stepchild may be reluctant to spend assets for the surviving spouse, because whatever is spent on that spouse comes out of the child's inheritance. Then what if stepparent gets remarried? How will the stepchild trustee react to that event? What if it turns out the stepchild liked the stepparent when his parent was living, but not so much afterwards?

Here is where the lawyer as co-trustee may provide an ideal solution. When one parent dies, the lawyer steps in as co-trustee with the surviving spouse. The lawyer helps the stepparent to invest for their own benefit as well as making sure the principal grows to offset inflation, for the benefit of the deceased spouse's heirs.

The stepparent in this case takes care of all their business privately with their lawyer. The trusts cannot be raided. These protections may also be extended for IRA and 401(k) money passing to the spouse through the use of the "IRA Contract". Surviving spouse agrees ahead of time that they will make an irrevocable designation of the deceased spouse's children as beneficiaries when the IRA is left to the surviving spouse, and further agrees that any withdrawals in excess of the required minimum distribution (RMD) may only be made on consent of the lawyer.

When the trust terms are read the deceased spouse's children are relieved by the protection that has been set up for them, have no concern about the stepparent's having sole control of the assets and the relationship between them may continue to grow and flourish.

QTIP, in connection with trusts, stands for "Qualified Terminable Interest Property". These trusts are ideal for those who are in second or later marriages and are confronted with balancing the needs of their surviving spouse when they die while still providing an inheritance for their children from a prior marriage.

Essentially, this type of trust continues free of estate tax for a surviving spouse, providing them with income for life (i.e. interest and dividends) and principal, if needed, with either the surviving spouse themselves or someone else in charge as trustee or both the spouse and someone else as co-trustees. The someone else may be another family member, a bank or trust company or a lawyer or other professional, such as an accountant. The financial advisor, while often a close confidant and long-serving professional, is not advised in cases where they are still handling the family finances due to a conflict of interest. In addition, many financial institutions prohibit their advisors from acting as trustees.

QTIP trusts allow the grantor (creator) of the trust to stipulate where the assets go after the surviving spouse dies, presumably to the grantor's children from a prior marriage.

QTIP trust assets are sheltered from any liabilities of the surviving spouse and professional management may be arranged. There are also major psychological and social benefits in that (1) the children from the prior marriage know that their inheritance is protected from being squandered or diverted, and (2) they may continue and even enhance their relationship with the surviving stepparent once the fear of being left out has been removed.

While the surviving spouse may legally act as sole trustee of the QTIP trust, for the foregoing social reasons this may not be advisable.

Some of the rules associated with a QTIP trust are that all income must be paid out to the surviving spouse every year, the spouse must be a US citizen, and there may be no other beneficiaries during the surviving spouse's lifetime.

12

Planning for Those Without Children

For singles and couples without children, the lawyer as co-trustee fulfills an entirely different function. In the couples setting, we are referring to the issues that arise after the first spouse dies. From an estate planning point of view, couples without children ultimately have the same issues as singles.

So whether you are single now or become one after your partner dies, your key issue is usually not planning for death, not who you are leaving it to and certainly not having a will. Your key issue is planning for disability. Should you be unable, at some point, to handle your financial and legal affairs due to accident or illness, who will take over? If you don't have a strong plan for disability, which eventually happens to about half of all people, you are at considerable risk of having the wrong person or a stranger take over your affairs. In the event of disability, virtually any interested party (hospital, doctor, lawyer, social worker, relative, etc.) may initiate a proceeding to have a legal guardian appointed for you. Once you enter into this bureaucratic process, usually involuntarily, it is difficult to extricate yourself and you lose precious control over your affairs. We often say you are only as strong as your back-up plan. If you have set up a living trust, you put yourself in charge now, but the trust says who takes over in the event of disability. You get the person or persons you have chosen, not a court appointed legal guardian, along with the many thousands of dollars in costs, and the associated stress, that such proceedings entail.

So, who should you choose? We recommend that you choose two people. One a friend or relative who is willing to undertake the responsibility, and knows you well, and then the lawyer as co-trustee. The lawyer will see to it that the trust is run properly and that all of your affairs are handled according to law. It takes a considerable amount of the anxiety, pressure and responsibility off of your friend or relative who has so kindly agreed to undertake this task but may be inexperienced. Further, you have two people signing off on all decisions, and everyone knows what two heads are better than. Not only is the possibility of a mistake being made greatly reduced, but it also eliminates the risk of misappropriation of assets. We are also mindful that one person, acting alone, may be influenced by someone else who you didn't choose.

In many cases, where clients do not have a friend or relative available for this purpose or where they do not want to burden anyone with the responsibility, the lawyer may act as sole trustee.

In our view, for singles and couples without children, planning for disability is more important than planning for death. In the case of disability, the lawyer as co-trustee may be an invaluable asset to the person without immediate family or who wishes to use an independent third party for other reasons.

13

Protecting Assets for Spendthrift Children

It's an estate planning epidemic. So many successful parents we meet have children who are poor at handling money, have not achieved significant success in life where they have any experience in handling money, or they simply refuse to grow up. What's a parent to do?

Enter what has been termed the greatest invention of English common law: the trust. Trusts are legal entities that may hold and use assets for a beneficiary (your son or daughter) but have them managed by a trustee (one of more responsible adults, including a professional trustee).

Historically, estate planning consisted of setting up a will and leaving everything to one's children in equal shares, "per stirpes".

The "per stirpes" is Latin for "by the roots", meaning that if any of the children predecease their parents then their share goes to their children, if any.

Today, however, adolescence lasts much longer than it used to. Some say that "30 is the new 20" and, anecdotally, we see much evidence of this. Another recent phenomenon is children coming back home to live with their parents, for many reasons, but often having to do with their inability to deal with the problems of life or the shrunken job market.

In light of the foregoing, and the fact that trusts, which have become as common as wills today, may continue for many years after the death of the parent, new planning options are available to clients.

For example, one popular plan of distribution is 20% at age thirty, one-half of the remaining balance at thirty-five and the remainder at forty. The theory here is that the child can get the 20% and spend it all, but they have to wait five years before they get one-half of what's left and then, finally, ten years later, when they have hopefully made their mistakes and matured somewhat, they still have about one-half of the inheritance left. A twist on this plan is 20% on the death of the parent, one-half of the remaining balance five years after the parent's death and the remainder ten years after the parent's death. This latter formula is often accompanied by a "cap". For example, upon attaining the age of fifty, any undistributed amounts shall then be distributed outright to the adult child beneficiary.

It is important to note here that assets left in the trust for delayed distribution are still available for the child's health, education, maintenance and support. Those assets are simply managed by the more experienced and mature trustee who makes decisions as to distribution of income and principal.

What if the parent wishes to "rule from the grave" and keep the assets in trust for the child's lifetime?

Let's say your son Richard is a problem. Your estate plan using a living trust would provide that upon your death or, if you have a spouse, upon the second death, Richard's share would go into The Richard Trust with perhaps a family member and your attorney as co-trustees. The Richard Trust continues for his lifetime, and the trustees would use the money for Richard's health, education, maintenance and support. The trust may help him start a business, buy a house or, alternatively, purchase a house for him. Then, upon his death, the trust would go to his children (at a stated age) or, if there are none, to his siblings or his nieces and nephews.

The "sprinkling", or "spray" trust is also often used in this context. Let's say Richard has two children and you are very concerned about them as well. You may set up a trust for Richard and his children and direct the trustee to "sprinkle" the income and principal amongst the beneficiaries, in equal or unequal amounts, whenever it is needed or will do the most good. So if one of Richard's children is accepted to Harvard, while the other goes to the local community college, the trust may help both. An added bonus with these trusts is that they keep the assets out of the hands of Richard's spouse who, in some cases, may be a large part of the financial problem.

For children in dire financial straits or perhaps headed in that general direction, the effects of a potential bankruptcy on the inheritance and estate administration must be addressed. What happens if your son or daughter files for bankruptcy within six months of the date of your death? The inherited assets are then available for their creditors. Nevertheless, by leaving assets to your son or daughter in a trust, giving the trustee discretion to distribute income and principal as the trustee sees fit, you may protect those assets from being lost in a subsequent bankruptcy proceeding.

There is much to consider concerning setting up a trust for an adult child, such as the pros and cons of naming siblings, other relatives, friends and professional advisors as trustees. Other factors are how long the trust should go on, what payments the trust should allow or disallow, and who the back-up trustees might be. All your choices have their issues which need to be fleshed out, with the help of an experienced attorney, so as to provide the plan that best suits your family's needs.

14

Planning for Same-Sex Couples

Same-sex couples face unique estate planning issues. Since Obergefell v. Hodges, same-sex marriages have been legal in all fifty states. Living trusts are often the estate planning vehicle of choice for the gay community for a number of reasons.

1. They provide for your partner to be able to handle your assets should you become disabled. Powers of attorney and health care proxies/living wills are documents that also help insure that your partner will be in charge of all legal, financial and medical decision-making in the event of disability, free of interference from other family members.

2. Will planning has fallen into disfavor because (a) wills are significantly easier to challenge than trusts (b) a notice of the

proceeding must be given to your closest legal heirs, providing them with an opportunity to object (c) the will is a public record, eliminating privacy, and (d) the legal process may be time consuming, possibly delaying the surviving partner's access to needed funds.

3. Simply putting your partner's name on your assets, or joint tenancy, seems to be a simple solution to many, until they learn of the pitfalls. First, for appreciated assets, such as stocks and real estate, there are tax disadvantages to receiving assets from a joint tenant. While inheriting from a will or trust at death eliminates taxable capital gains for the survivor, joint tenancy only eliminates one-half of those capital gains since you are only "inheriting" one-half of the property. Secondly, you may be exposed to the debts and liabilities of your partner. Thirdly, you lose control over where the assets go after your surviving partner dies. Perhaps you may want to provide for your partner for life, but state where the unused assets will go after he or she passes. Finally, once you make your assets joint with your partner, you may have more difficulty in getting those assets back in the event of a divorce or break up in the relationship.

4. If either or both partners have children, care must be taken as to how those children are provided for on the death of the first partner. Many of the same considerations apply as in second marriage planning (Chapter 11), such as what they will receive when their parent dies and what they will receive when the surviving partner dies, as well as how their rights will be protected in the interim.

5. Funeral and burial arrangements are often contentious matters. Proper legal documents will allow you to designate the person you

wish to have control of the arrangements as well as providing in writing the specific type of funeral and burial that you may wish.

6. As same-sex couples age, there may be good reasons not to marry for Medicaid planning purposes. Whereas for married couples the combined assets of the couple are available for the care of the ill spouse, such is not the case for unmarried couples -- so your assets are legally protected from your partner's cost of care. Further, while married couples who wish to plan ahead with a Medicaid Asset Protection Trust (MAPT) may not name each other as trustee, such is not the case for unmarried couples. So if you wish to protect your home and life savings from long-term care costs, and cannot obtain long-term care insurance for any reason, you may each establish MAPT's for each other and need not go outside the relationship to put someone else in charge in order to protect your assets.

In our experience, crafting an estate plan for the same-sex couple that is thought through, addressing all the potential social, legal, financial, health and tax issues, is a loving act that provides peace of mind knowing your choices will be legally protected and honored.

15

Planning Issues for Women

When Husband Handled the Finances

While women and men have many issues in common, some of these issues tend to affect women more deeply. For example, in the case of the death or disability of a spouse, it is more often the surviving wife who is unfamiliar with handling the family finances. In the course of planning for such a couple, it is wise to find a financial advisor that the wife can turn to. Ideally, this relationship should be developed over the years while the husband is living, so that there is a seamless transfer of decision-making. Where such a relationship with a financial advisor is absent, one of the financially savvy children may be named as a co-trustee with the surviving wife or, should none of the children be suitable for that role, the attorney as co-trustee may be considered.

Children from Prior Marriages

With the increase in second marriages, many women have children from previous marriages. How will those children fare should a wife die first? This dynamic may be complicated by the fact that there are children from the second marriage as well as the first. Here, we consider making partial gifts to the children of the first marriage, who are generally older, on the wife's death. The balance of the assets may be kept in trust for the surviving husband, providing for him during his lifetime and, on his death, paying out to the wife's children from the second marriage. Alternatively, wife's entire estate may be held in trust and pay out to all of her children in equal shares after the husband dies.

In the second marriage context, what about the husband's children from a prior marriage? If the wife is going to be financially dependent on some or all of his assets after his death, she may want to avoid the situation when one or more of the husband's children are in charge of the money after he dies. Here, the pitfalls are many. They may not wish to distribute principal to her, feeling that the funds are coming out of their inheritance. She may find out that they do not care for her personally, even though this was not apparent when their father was alive. They may disapprove of her subsequent remarriage. We have recommended to many women clients that they choose the lawyer to act as co-trustee with her after a husband's death. This way, the conflict of interest that the husband's children have is eliminated and she may handle her personal and financial business privately with her own lawyer. Second marriage planning, more fully discussed in Chapter 11, is particularly important for women.

Medicaid Issues for Women

Since women tend to live longer than men, they make up the majority of nursing home residents. Planning to protect assets, especially the family's home, from being lost to the costs of long-term care, is essential. Medicaid Asset Protection Trusts (MAPT's) should be put into place when a husband dies. While the home was exempt from Medicaid when the spouse was living, it becomes an available resource, required to be "spent down" if a single person requires long-term care.

What if it is a second marriage and the couple has executed a pre-nuptial agreement? Many are surprised to learn that they are financially responsible for the cost of their husband's care despite the prenuptial agreement. Medicaid is not bound by that agreement and considers the combined assets of the couple to be available for the care of the ill spouse, regardless of whose name those assets are in. Before contemplating a second marriage later in life, especially where the man is older, a woman should determine whether her intended has long-term care insurance or, if not, is willing and able to purchase that insurance so that her assets are protected. If he is unable or unwilling to purchase long-term care insurance, she should consider setting up a MAPT for herself to protect her assets.

Women's Role as Caregivers

Fair or not, women tend to care for their aging parents far more often than men. What if a woman has to take unpaid leave from employment for this purpose? Caregiver Agreements, discussed in more detail later, are designed to compensate the daughter for the job of caring and sometimes boarding her aging parents. Consideration should be given to having siblings agree to the terms of the Caregiver Agreement to avoid misunderstandings later on. There may be the need for a "lump-sum" distribution to the daughter to improve her home or put an addition on for the parents to reside in. The parents may wish to acquire life rights to stay in that home in exchange for the lump sum payment. Discussion should occur as to whether some or all of the lump sum will be considered a gift to be subtracted out of the daughter's ultimate share of the inheritance.

Where the responsibility lies with the daughter caregiver, we recommend that she be named as the agent under the parent's power of attorney as well as the agent for medical decisions under the health care proxy and/or living will. Wherever possible, we advise against these powers residing with a sibling who lives far away. It is difficult for the daughter who bears the bulk of the responsibility not to have the powers to adequately discharge that responsibility, not to mention the annoyance of being second-guessed by a sibling who is not there day-to-day to see what is going on.

Medicaid Asset Protection Trust (MAPT) planning should also be considered for the parents at this time. Even the strongest and most well intentioned caregiver may ultimately find themselves overwhelmed and unable to cope with the burden of care giving. Other risks for the caregiver may be (1) a health issue or other crisis that arises for her or a member of her family, or (2) the parent requiring a level of skilled care that is beyond the daughter's ability to provide. In the foregoing situations, a nursing home stay may become inevitable. The daughter should take all steps from the very beginning to protect parents' assets since, being in charge, she will later be answerable to her siblings for the actions she may or may not have taken. Here, reliance on the elder law attorney's advice may well insulate her from later claims.

16

Disinheriting A Spouse

New York law prevents spouses from being disinherited. Instead, a spouse who is disinherited may go to court and claim their "elective share" which is the greater of fifty thousand dollars or one-third of the estate.

Questions often arise as what the "estate" of the deceased spouse consists of. Naturally, any assets in the decedent's name only and listed in the probate court proceeding apply. Other assets, known as "testamentary substitutes" because they do not pass by will, and which against which the spouse may make their claim are: bank accounts, investment accounts and retirement accounts with named beneficiaries other than the spouse or, similarly, those same asset if they have a joint owner other than the spouse. An exception would be if the other joint owner had made contributions to the joint account and then as to the contributions only.

Gifts made within one year of death are also available for the elective share claim. Oddly enough, life insurance is not considered a testamentary substitute although annuities are.

A valid and enforceable prenuptial or postnuptial agreement can prevent the spouse from claiming an elective share. Another exception is "abandonment". In the will of the late Cars rock group's lead singer, Ric Ocasek, he disinherited his spouse, model Pauline Porizkova, claiming she had abandoned him. However, a simple claim of abandonment is not proof of abandonment and she was reportedly able to settle with his estate saying "They were very fair. They gave me what is mine under New York state law, and we're done".

For those who die "intestate" in New York, i.e. without a will, the rules are different. In those cases, the surviving spouse is entitled to the whole estate if there were no children, being in that case the closest relative, or if there were children of the marriage, then fifty thousand dollars plus one-half of the estate.

Keep in mind that the elective share is not automatic. The surviving spouse has to go to court to get it unless the estate chooses to settle the claim.

17

Avoiding Guardianship in New York

For the ever-increasing number of those who become legally incapacitated later in life (i.e. unable to handle their legal and financial affairs) having a legal guardian appointed looms as a distinct possibility.

A guardianship proceeding may be commenced by a hospital, nursing home, assisted living residence, family member or a professional involved in the affairs of the "alleged incapacitated person" or "AIP". These proceedings arise for various reasons such as the facility looking to secure payment or a family member or professional finding that the AIP is either not handling their affairs well or is being taken advantage of financially.

Once the proceeding is commenced a vast bureaucratic process begins to unfold. Notice of the proceeding and of the date and location of any hearings are sent to all interested parties, including all immediate family members.

The court appoints a court evaluator to meet with the AIP, determine the nature and extent of the disability and write a report to the judge. The judge will also appoint a lawyer to represent the AIP in the proceeding and sometimes adult children will want their own lawyers to represent their interests.

The judge decides on who the legal guardian will be and it often ends up being a stranger to the family. Some judges feel that the AIP's children should not be guardian due to a conflict – that whatever they spend on the AIP is coming out of their inheritance. Other reasons for not choosing one of the AIP's adult children are sibling rivalry or inability (in the judge's opinion) to handle the responsibility.

Guardianship proceedings are expensive, time-consuming and highly stressful to all involved, including the AIP. Trusts avoid guardianship by providing privately who will handle your legal and financial affairs should you become legally incapacitated. Having a trust means you will have those in charge who you know and trust instead of the possibility of a court appointed stranger.

18

Business Succession Planning

While ninety percent of American businesses are family owned, only about thirty percent of them continue to the next generation. Half of those again make it to the third generation. The most common reason: lack of a business succession plan.

There are many reasons owners fail to plan. In addition to confronting the issues of age and mortality, the business owner also faces potentially giving up his or her life's work – often a venture started, nurtured and grown by him or her over many years.

Business succession planning should start while the entrepreneur is young enough to spend time mentoring the next generation, be it family or otherwise. Around the age of sixty-five should allow enough time, say five to ten years, for the process to begin and develop.

One of the first things the owner should consider is what to do with the new found time as others take on more of the burden of running the business. Other goals to achieve will help the business owner transition to a new life that does not center around the former work and lifestyle.

A business plan should be created, or an existing one modified, to take into account the reality of the succession, ideally with input from the successors. This will allow for the personal feelings, ambitions and goals of everyone concerned to be accounted for.
Professional advisors will need to be consulted – accountants for business evaluations and tax planning, lawyers for estate planning and to prepare agreements and financial advisors to determine investment and income strategies for the departing owner and their spouse.

Two of the methods used to transfer ownership are as follows:

1. Gifting using the annual exclusion. Currently at $17,000 per year and indexed to inflation, a couple who files a joint tax return may annually elect to "split" the gift and give $34,000 worth of stock in the company to each child (or any other person for that matter). In addition to the annual exclusion, each spouse may gift about thirteen million dollars over their lifetimes. A gift tax return must be filed but no tax is due since the client is merely using a portion of their estate tax exemption during their lifetime. So, for example, if you gift out $3,000,000 today, you only have $10,000,000 left to gift tax-free upon your death. If you feel the business is going to appreciate rapidly in the future, now might be a good time to use some or all of the lifetime gift tax exemption to get the business, or

property owned by it, out of your estate, to avoid potentially heavy estate taxes later.

If the owner feels that the successors may not be ready to receive substantial portions of the business, but still wishes to move assets out of their name now for tax purposes, irrevocable trusts may be used. These trusts may then transfer more assets to the successors at a time or series of times in the future.

2. The major tool used in effectuating a business-succession plan is the "buy-sell agreement". The buy-sell agreement stipulates that the seller must sell and the buyer must buy, at a pre-determined value (adjusted from time to time between the parties), and upon a predetermined event. Events triggering the provisions of the agreement include, but are not limited to, retirement, disability or death.

There are many forms of buy-sell agreements. The most common is the cross-purchase agreement whereby the remaining shareholders or partners, as the case may be, agree to purchase the departing owner's share of the enterprise upon retirement, disability or death. The agreement is typically funded with insurance for death or disability but, for retirement, the remaining owners will typically have to fund the agreement through the profits of the business. Upon death, the insurance may still be used to confer a remaining benefit on the departing owner's heirs. The retiring owner's retirement income interest may be secured with a private annuity or a promissory note executed by the business itself and perhaps personally guaranteed as well. The foregoing strategies may also include survivor's benefits for the owner's spouse.

In cases where there are no other shareholders or partners, key employees should be considered as potential buyers under the agreement since they will best be able to run the business and generate the income needed to fund the owner's retirement and/or pay the insurance premiums.

With the right amount of thought and expertise brought to bear on the problem of succession, the business will more likely be one of the few that confers benefits on the owner's family for generations to come – leaving a lasting legacy to his or her dedication, hard work and foresight.

19

Prenuptial Agreements

Prenuptial agreements ("prenups") are contracts entered into by a couple before marriage setting out the rights of the parties in the event of divorce or death. Less common is the postnuptial agreement, with similar terms, but executed by the parties after marriage.

Who signs these types of agreements and why? Often couples marrying for the second or more time will have children and/or substantial assets at the time of remarriage. They may wish to insure that all or some of their assets go to their children and not to the new spouse, who may have children and assets of their own. Even with a will which leaves everything to one's children, without a prenup the surviving spouse is legally entitled to claim one third of the deceased spouse's estate. Having been married before, these couples know that sometimes things do not work out and wish to simplify matters in the event of a divorce, including whether or not alimony will be payable.

In the prenup there must be full disclosure of each other's assets so that each party knows what they are giving up. A necessary component is a schedule whereby each party sets out a list of their separate property, i.e. what they owned prior to entering into the marriage. The agreement then sets out the division of property in the event of divorce as well as the inheritance rights between the parties. While prenups often provide that neither party will inherit from the other, it is not unusual for the parties to partially waive those provisions after a few years and execute a will or trust leaving assets to the spouse despite the prenup. Other ways to leave assets to the spouse are by making some assets joint or naming the spouse as beneficiary on IRA's, investments, bank accounts, annuities or insurance policies. The prenup may also contain a "sunset provision" that it expires after the parties have been married for a set number of years.

When there is great economic disparity between the parties, or one of them owns a business, the wealthy spouse may want to protect themselves and, similarly, the less well off spouse will want to establish what they will receive in assets and/or alimony in the event of divorce. If there are business partners of one of the spouses, they may want protection so that the new spouse does not become a partner in the business by way of inheritance.

In our experience, prenups do not work well with younger couples about to enter into a first marriage. They are considered unromantic and usually the young couple does not have sufficient assets to be concerned. While some of them may be coming into substantial inheritances, the invention of the Inheritance Protection Trust (IPT) has solved this problem. Parents may now leave the inheritance to a trust that protects the assets for their son or daughter in the event of divorce and pass it by blood, instead of by marriage. In the event of death, the child's spouse has no right to make a claim against a trust set up by a third party.

A key advantage of the Inheritance Protection Trust over the prenup is that no disclosure is required. The child who has the IPT does not need to disclose what assets are in the trust or even that the trust exists.

20

Contesting a Will

In order to contest a will, the objectant must have "standing", meaning they would legally be entitled to a share or a greater share of the estate if the will was declared invalid. "Standing" alone, however, is insufficient. There must also be grounds for contesting as provided below.

1. **Undue Influence:** Independent caregivers and caregiver children who end up being named primary beneficiaries under the will are often scrutinized for having prevailed upon the decedent to leave them the lion's share of the estate. The various means alleged may be physical or mental abuse, threats or isolation of the disabled person. Even non-caregivers who had influence over mom or dad may be challenged where they end up with more than their fair share. As with any court proceedings, proof of the claim will need to be made.

2. Improper Execution: The formalities for executing a will must be strictly observed. The formalities include that the witnesses believed the decedent was of sound mind, memory and understanding. There must be two witnesses who signed in the presence of the testator and of each other. The testator must declare in front of the witnesses that they read the will, understood it, declare that it is their last will and testament and approve of the two witnesses to act as witnesses to the will.

3. Incapacity: Even if the witnesses testify they believed that the testator was capable to sign the will, a challenge may still be made that the person was not able to read the will due to a defect of sight or was unable to understand either the will, what property they owned or who their heirs were, due to mental incapacity. These latter claims will require medical proof.

Challengers should be wary of the "no-contest clause". This provides that any benefit the challenging party would have received under the will is forfeited if the challenge is unsuccessful. If the gift was substantial, even though not an equal share, the no-contest clause is a powerful disincentive to contest the will.

21

The Young Family Estate Plan (YFEP)

It is not unusual for parents of young children to overlook the need for a Will, Power of Attorney and Health Care Proxy/Living Will – what we term a "Young Family Estate Plan" (YFEP). Many feel they don't have enough assets yet or that everything will automatically go to their spouse and then he or she will take care of things.

One of the main reasons for young families to plan is to insure that should something happen to the parents, their children will continue to thrive and reach their full potential.

Here are problems that may occur for young parents who fail to have a YFEP:

(1) If both parents die in a common disaster, then the courts will decide on the legal guardian for your children without consideration of who you would have wanted.

(2) If any assets were in husband's or wife's name alone, and failed to name spouse as beneficiary, then a court proceeding will be required to name an "administrator" of your estate and New York law decides who gets which assets. If you have a spouse and children, the first $50,000 goes to your spouse and rest is divided 50% to your spouse and 50% to your children. However, if your children are under age eighteen they are minors and may not represent themselves in court. In that case, the court will appoint a second lawyer to represent the interests of your children, at your expense.

(3) Assets that go to your children as a result of what happened in (2) above, or if the parents die together in a common disaster, must be distributed to the children at age eighteen, since they are then legally considered "adults". Until that time, the court decides who will be in charge of your assets, and how the money will be used for your children.

(4) A YFEP involves not just a Will, but also Power of Attorney and Health Care Proxy/Living Will. Should your spouse have an accident or illness rendering them incapacitated, you will be unable to handle their legal and financial affairs (such as selling or refinancing the house or drawing funds from their accounts) or to make end-of-life health care decisions for them, such as terminating life support should the need arise. Without these basic documents, you would be forced to petition the courts to be appointed as your spouse's legal guardian – an expensive and time-consuming legal process putting the courts, instead of you, in charge. There is the added risk that the court may decide against you as legal guardian and appoint someone else, or that another family member may challenge you as guardian and seek the guardianship themselves.

With a YFEP you will be able to:

A. Insure that all of your spouse's assets go to you and not half to your children if your spouse dies unexpectedly.

B. Choose who you want as legal guardian for your children as well as how your money will be used for your children and at what age they will receive your assets. We usually recommend putting a trusted relative or friend in charge until they are at least age thirty.

C. Avoid guardianship proceedings should your spouse have a disabling accident or illness and have the legal documents you need to handle your spouse's legal, financial and medical affairs.

Need for Insurance

A YFEP includes life and disability insurance reviews and recommendations so in the event your spouse dies or becomes disabled you will have the financial resources to continue to raise your children. Most young families are woefully unprepared financially should disaster strike. We make sure that your or your lost spouse's economic value is replaced so that your family can go forward confidently into the future.
"Special Needs" and other Situations

A YFEP also addresses the complications involved with "special needs" children (Chapter 9), single and divorced parents, and second marriages with blended families.

FINANCIAL AND TAX ASPECTS
OF ESTATE PLANNING

22

The SECURE Act and Your IRA

The SECURE Act governs distributions from IRA's and other retirement plans. After the death of the account holder, most named beneficiaries are required to take the funds out over ten years.

The inherited IRA beneficiary must take minimum distributions for the first nine years, based on the life expectancy of the beneficiary. More may be taken, and taxes will be based on that amount. The way the minimum distribution works is as follows. Let's say the beneficiary has a life expectancy of forty years when the account holder dies. In the year following the account holder's death they must take one-fortieth, the following year one-thirty-ninth, and so on until year ten when they are required to take the retirement account balance in full.

There are a few exceptions to the ten year rule. Spouses may roll the inherited IRA into an IRA of their own and continue it for their own lifetime -- generally waiting until they are 73 to start taking required minimum distributions (RMD's) unless they need the funds earlier.

Disabled or chronically ill beneficiaries are entitled to the "stretch-out" of payments for life. So, in the above example, they would not have to liquidate the account in year ten but instead would be able to take the distributions over the full forty years.

Non-spouses less than ten years younger are also entitled to the stretch-out. This might be a sibling or a life partner.

Correctly prepared trusts may be beneficiaries of your IRA's subject to the ten year rule. However, Special Needs Trusts get the exception of the stretch-out. These trusts may be set up for special needs children and grandchildren.

One strategy for getting the highly valuable lifetime stretch would be to leave the IRA to the Special Needs Trust and other assets to the other children. The purchase of life insurance, with premiums being paid from RMD's during the account holder's lifetime, may be used to make up for any shortfall in the shares to the other children.

23

Leaving an IRA to a Trust

An IRA may not be transferred to a trust without causing the whole IRA to be taxed. The "I" in IRA stands for "individual" -- it must be owned by a single person. In practice, there is no need to transfer an IRA to a trust since IRA's avoid probate by having a "designated beneficiary" and the principal of an IRA is exempt from being "spent down" for your long-term care needs. However, an IRA may be left to a trust. In other words you may name a trust as a designated beneficiary of an IRA.

There are many reasons why one would want to leave an IRA to a trust. The beneficiary may be a minor, they may be irresponsible, have substance or alcohol abuse issues, learning disabled, special needs, dominated by a spouse, facing divorce or bankruptcy, or you may simply want to control where the IRA money goes if your designated beneficiary dies before the IRA is completely distributed. Similarly an IRA is often left to the Inheritance Protection Trust to protect it from your child's divorces or creditors and to keep the asset in the bloodline.

There are two types of trusts that may be named a beneficiary of an IRA -- "conduit" trusts and "accumulation" trusts. A conduit trust simply acts as a conduit of the ten year payout under the SECURE Act. In other words, whatever is taken from the IRA must be distributed immediately to the trust beneficiary, the trust acting as a conduit only.

An accumulation trust will more often be a better choice for the purposes described above. These trusts allow the trustee to keep the IRA proceeds in the trust and use them "as needed" for the benefit of the trust beneficiary or group of beneficiaries.

A final word on the payout. Many were disappointed that the "stretch" provisions, allowing a beneficiary to take the IRA distributions over their lifetime, were eliminated by the SECURE Act. However, the beneficiary usually only has to take very small distributions for the first nine years, allowing for virtually a full ten years of tax-free growth on the whole IRA.

Word to the wise: it is a good idea to have an experienced elder law estate planning attorney handle the retitling of the decedent's IRA to avoid a taxable event from occurring.

24

Tax Issues on Death

When a person dies, the executor of a will or the trustee of a trust has certain responsibilities to settle and close the estate, including addressing tax issues.

Executors and trustees, as fiduciaries of the estate, must identify, manage and protect estate assets, pay off creditors, distribute the remaining estate to beneficiaries, and file tax returns as needed. Any of the following possible federal and state tax returns may be required. Fiduciaries are held to a high standard - - that of the utmost good faith.

Personal Income Tax Return. If the deceased person (called a decedent) had an obligation to file a personal income tax return in the year of his or her death, then the fiduciary must file a personal tax return for the decedent.

Estate or Trust Income Tax Return. The fiduciary may also have to file an income tax return for the probate estate or the trust estate. From the date of death, any income generated by any of the decedent's probate or trust assets is income of the estate or the trust. If the estate or trust income is $600 or less from the date of death, then no return is required.

Estate Tax Return. The fiduciary may also need to file an estate tax return, but only if the decedent's estate is worth more than the estate tax exemption amount. The federal exemption amount is $12.92 million per person for 2023. The New York State estate tax exemption is $6.58 million.

Many rules, deadlines, exemptions and exceptions apply to income tax and estate tax reporting requirements. It is important to consult with a professional to properly govern the process and possibly plan ahead to avoid costly tax liability. For example, New York does not have a gift tax and by planning ahead gifts can be made so that once a person dies, their estate will be under the New York estate tax limit. However, the sooner you act the better, since if you die within three years of making the gift, New York has a "claw-back" that brings the gift back into your estate.

25

"Disclaimer Trusts" for Taxable Estates

For couples with taxable estates, "disclaimer trusts" are commonly used today to allow the surviving spouse greater flexibility in optimizing estate tax savings.

Here's how they work. Each spouse sets up their own revocable living trust. Husband and wife are co-trustees of his trust, using his social security number and, vice versa, they are both co-trustees of her trust with her social security number. Let's say husband dies first. His trust says "leave everything to my wife except that, whatever she disclaims, i.e. refuses to take, will remain in my trust". The disclaimer is a legal document that lists the assets disclaimed and their value. Wife remains as trustee on husband's trust after he dies and may use the funds in his trust for her health, maintenance and support. She may also remove 5% of the trust every year for any reason or $5,000, whichever is greater.

The reason wife is limited to health, maintenance and support is that if she had the right to take whatever she wanted at any time for any reason, the IRS would say that she had complete control of the funds and would then seek to tax those funds in her estate. The access for health, maintenance and support, however, is sufficiently broad so as not to cause a problem for her. She may also continue to buy, sell and trade assets in the husband's trust. This trust continues for her lifetime and pays out to the beneficiaries at her death along with her own trust.

Husband's social security number died with him so his trust took out a trust tax identification number (TTID) when he died and reported as a separate taxpayer during her lifetime. It is not includible in her estate. Indeed, what has happened is that husband's trust was settled on his death and left to his beneficiaries, but subject to wife's lifetime use and enjoyment of the trust assets.

The benefit of the disclaimer is that it allows the wife to decide (or the husband if wife dies first) how much to leave in the deceased spouse's trust based on her age, her health and the tax laws at that future time. On her death, his trust passes estate tax-free to the children, regardless of how much it may have grown.

26

New York and Federal Estate Taxes

The current exemption from New York estate taxes is 6.58 million, indexed for inflation. For the majority of our clients this presents no issue – their estates will never approach the exemption.

However, for the fortunate few who have assets, including life insurance, that may exceed roughly six and a half million dollars, there is a significant tax liability. Changes in New York estate tax law in the last few years introduced a "fiscal cliff". Whereas formerly New York only taxed the amount over the exemption, if you exceed the limit today (by a mere 5%) they tax the whole estate. You're over the cliff!

The tax is surprisingly large. On a roughly seven million dollar estate, the taxes payable to New York exceed five hundred thousand dollars. An estate over ten million would owe over a million in estate tax.

These New York estate taxes are avoidable if you have a spouse and you create an estate plan using two trusts, described in Chapter 25 "Disclaimer Trusts". Another way to avoid the fiscal cliff is to use the "Santa Clause" providing that you gift to charities of your choice all amounts over the exemption. Gifts to charities are deductible from estate taxes.

While the Federal estate tax exemption of 12.92 million is "portable", i.e. if the first spouse doesn't use their exemption or any part of it, it passes to the surviving spouse, New York does not allow for portability. It's use it or lose it.

The Federal exemption is expected to be reduced from the 12.92 million exemption passed by the Trump administration to the 6.58 million that New York uses, at the end of 2025. For larger estates, there remains a planning opportunity by making gifts while the higher exemption is in place. You may use any of your estate tax exemptions to make gifts while you are living. These gifts are reported to the IRS and get subtracted from what you may give at death.

One added attraction to gifting is that New York does not tax gifts -- so that gifts also avoid onerous estate taxes at death. There is a minor exception that gifts made within three years of the death of the donor are brought back into the donor's estate for estate tax purposes.

27

Mistakes with Beneficiary Designations

A common estate planning mistake occurs with beneficiary designations. If done correctly, the beneficiary designation avoids probate and transfers the asset directly to the beneficiary. If you make a mistake on the beneficiary designation, your plan may be at risk from creditors, former spouses, and miscellaneous relatives who may fight for their share. Following are some common mistakes and misconceptions that lead to problems with beneficiary designations:

If you fail to name a beneficiary or name someone that is deceased, the asset will usually go to probate. If you have a will, the will names the beneficiaries. If you don't have a will, the state intestacy (what happens if there is no will) law determines the beneficiaries.

Naming your "estate" as a beneficiary on retirement funds is not recommended. When you list your estate as the beneficiary, it means the asset will have to be probated. '

A thorough review of all assets, goals and desires is important in a comprehensive elder law estate plan. However, the following recommendations may avoid serious problems with beneficiary designations:

- Name a primary beneficiary.
- Name a contingent beneficiary in case the primary beneficiary dies before you.
- Do not name your estate as a beneficiary.
- Review beneficiary forms at least every three years
- Update your forms to reflect life changes such as a birth, death, marriage or divorce.
- Every time you change a form send it to the institution holding the account and ask them to acknowledge receipt of the change. Keep a copy for yourself.

Keep in mind that beneficiary designations simply avoid probate. They do not keep assets in the bloodline for your grandchildren or protect those assets from long-term care costs. In order to keep assets in the bloodline, an Inheritance Protection Trust (IPT) is used. To protect assets from long-term care costs, a Medicaid Asset Protection Trust (MAPT) is required.

28

Income Taxation of Trusts

Revocable living trusts, where the grantor (creator) and the trustee (manager) are the same person, use the grantor's social security number and are not required to file an income tax return. All income and capital gains taxes are reported on the individual's Form 1040.

Irrevocable living trusts come in two main varieties, "grantor" and "non-grantor" trusts. Non-grantor trusts are often used by the wealthy to give assets away during their lifetime and for all income and capital gains taxes to be paid either by the trust or the trust beneficiary but not by them. Gifts to non-grantor trusts are reported to the IRS but are rarely taxable. Currently, the annual exclusion is $17,000 per person per year to as many people as you wish. However, if you go over the $17,000 to any one person you must report the gift to Uncle Sam, but they merely subtract the excess gift from the $12,920,000 each person is allowed to give at death. Most of our clients are "comfortably under" as we like to say. These gifts then grow estate tax-free to the recipient.

Grantor trusts, such as the Medicaid Asset Protection Trust (MAPT), are designed to get the assets out of your name for Medicaid purposes but keep them in your name for tax purposes. You continue to receive income from the MAPT and pay income tax the same as before. The MAPT files an "informational return" (Form 1041) telling the IRS that all the income is passing through to you.

Gifts to non-grantor trusts take the grantor's "basis" for calculating capital gains taxes on sale, i.e. what the grantor originally paid and, if real estate, plus any capital improvements.

In the grantor trust, however, no gift is made on the transfer to the trust because the grantor reserves the right to change who they leave it to on death. The gift is therefore said to be "incomplete" until death and is therefore includible in the grantor's estate. Assets in the grantor's estate receive a "stepped-up basis". Instead of the grantor's original basis, the heirs get the date of death value as the basis, resulting in capital gains taxes being due only on gains arising from the date of death to the date of sale, if any.

29

Capital Gains Tax Tips

Your "basis" for calculating capital gains taxes is what you paid for the stock or the real estate. For real estate, the basis gets raised by the amount of any capital improvements you make to the property. When you sell your primary residence you may exclude the first $500,000 of gain if you're a couple or $250,000 if you're single. The $500,000 exclusion for a couple get extended for a sale occurring up to two years after a spouse dies.

For gifts you receive of appreciated stock or real estate during the donor's lifetime, no capital gains tax is payable, however the donee receives the donor's basis. It is generally considered better to wait, if possible, and pass the gift to the donee at death, due to the "stepped-up basis". The basis of any inherited property is "stepped-up" to date of death value. If the property is sold within six months of the date of death, then the sale price is deemed to be the date of death value.

If the property is going to be held for some time it is helpful to get date of death values to establish the new basis. For real estate, this means getting an appraisal from a licensed real estate appraiser (not a real estate broker!). For stocks, you simply ask the company holding the stocks to provide this information.

When a spouse dies with jointly held property, there is a half of a step-up -- the deceased spouse's half gets stepped-up to date of death value, while the surviving spouse has the original basis. However, for a primary residence the capital gains tax exclusions discussed in the first paragraph of this chapter continue to apply.

With combined Federal and New York capital gains taxes reaching about 30%, it is essential to look at holding onto appreciated property until death (especially if you have taken depreciation on the property which can lower your basis to zero) and to look carefully at the estate plan to see if property should be transferred to a surviving spouse to get another step-up on the second death.

30

Cashing in Your Life Insurance Policy

Everyone knows that you may surrender a life insurance policy at any time for the "cash surrender value". However, a better option may be a "life settlement" which pays more than the cash surrender value.

In a life settlement, you sell the policy to a third party instead of cashing it in. Here, the payment will be something greater than the cash surrender value but less than the death benefit. The buyer assumes the policy, pays the premiums and receives the death benefit.

There are many reasons why people want to cash in their policy. Paying the premiums have become a burden, they no longer need or want the death benefit or the money is needed for some other purpose.

There are some tax advantages to cashing in as well. Any money paid into the policy as premiums comes back to the seller tax-free (since the money used to pay the premiums was already taxed).
The purchaser of the policy will determine the amount they are willing to pay for the policy based on the amount, if any, of the cash surrender value and the age and health of the seller. Since there are numerous companies out there you may "shop around" for the best offering. Some companies offer a "life settlement calculator" where you may go online, plug in all your information, and receive a quote within twenty-four hours.

You may hear of the term "viatical settlement" when exploring the issue of whether or not to cash in your policy. Viatical settlements generally pay more than life settlements but are limited to terminally ill policy holders with less than two years of life expectancy as determined by a medical professional.

Finally, if you want to do the best you can with your policy, but do not have the time or inclination to shop around, there are "life settlement brokers" who, for a fee, will do the shopping for you

31

Reverse Mortgages

We have long been advocates of the reverse mortgage, an underutilized tool for seniors in need of additional retirement income.

Baby boomers as a group are currently between the ages of 58 and 76 years old. They tend to have lower savings rates than their parents, fewer pension and retirement plans, have experienced many years of lower interest rates and are facing considerably longer life expectancies.

Reverse mortgages are available to those 62 and older. No repayments are due until the last of the borrowers dies or the home is sold. Heirs have up to twelve months to sell the home, refinance the home or buy it themselves. You can never owe more than the house is worth so if the property is upside down the heirs can simply walk away. On the other hand, if the equity in the home exceeds the loan amount, the heirs keep the excess proceeds.

Reverse mortgage loans are generally tax-free for up to 70% of the equity. While there are no loan payments, the homeowner remains responsible for taxes, insurance and upkeep on the home. Loans may be taken as (1) a lump sum, (2) a line of credit; or (3) a stream of income. They are often used to pay off existing mortgages in order to eliminate mortgage payments and gain more disposable income.

Oddly enough, there may be some benefit to taking out a reverse mortgage closer to the age of 62. This allows the use of a relatively small portion of the reverse mortgage loan to fund life and long-term care insurance to both (a) protect the client's assets from the cost of long-term care, and (b) to replace the money taken out of the home with the tax-free proceeds of life insurance upon death. Those life insurance proceeds may also be used to pay off the reverse mortgage and keep the home.

For those looking for retirement alternatives, a reverse mortgage may allow for the purchase of a second home and the adoption of a "snowbird" lifestyle or it may allow for the purchase of an income-producing investment property. It may also be used to help adult children in need as an advance on their inheritance.

THE SOCIAL SIDE OF ESTATE PLANNING

32

Good Reasons to Plan Your Estate

1. Makes sure your estate goes to whom you want, when you want, the way you want. Most estate plans leave the assets to the next generation outright (i.e., in their hands) in equal shares. However, with a little bit of thought on your part, and some guidance from an experienced elder law estate planning attorney, you may dramatically improve the way your estate is ultimately distributed. For example, you may delay large bequests until children or grandchildren are older or give it to them in stages so that they have the chance to make some mistakes with the money without jeopardizing the whole inheritance. Similarly, you may place conditions on receipt of money such as "only upon graduation with a bachelor's degree" or "only to be used to purchase an annuity to provide a lifetime income for the beneficiary". The possibilities of course, are endless.

2. Allows you to give back to the people and places that have helped you. Again, most people leave their assets to their children in equal shares. Yet time and again we see children who really don't need the money or, unfortunately, don't deserve it. Even when they do need and deserve it, there is a place for remembering those people and institutions who have helped make you what you are today.

3. It proves stewardship by showing your family that you cared enough to plan for them. When you put time, thought and effort into planning your affairs it sends a powerful message to your loved ones. You are saying that you handled the matter with care and diligence. This will reflect itself in how the money is received, invested and spent by your heirs.

4. Saves your heirs legal fees, taxes and time in settling your affairs. Everyone understands and wants to save fees and taxes, but what about saving time? By planning ahead with trusts instead of wills, you may abbreviate the settlement process, thus aiding the grieving process by allowing families to heal more quickly and get on with their lives. In addition, while assets are tied up in an estate proceeding, valuable investment opportunities may be lost or additional expenses incurred, such as having to maintain a home.

5. Protects your assets from being eaten up by long-term care costs. No estate plan is complete without a plan to protect it from having to "spend down" your assets if you need care at home or a nursing home. If you don't qualify for long-term care insurance, due to medical or economic reasons, you should consider setting up trusts to protect your assets from long-term care costs.

6. Allows you to protect the inheritance from children's divorces, lawsuits and creditors. With middle class people often leaving hundreds of thousands of dollars to their children, doesn't it make sense to protect the inheritance from the high rate of divorce? By leaving assets to your children in an Inheritance Protection Trust, you may not only protect them from a divorce but, in many cases, also from creditors in the event your son or daughter ever gets sued.

7. Makes sure your estate will pass by blood instead of by marriage. Most estate plans leave the money to the children. So let's say that you have left $500,000 to your son and $500,000 to your daughter. Now if they die (remember this is after you're gone) who inherits from them? In many cases it's your son-in-law or daughter-in-law. Can they get remarried and share your $500,000 with a complete stranger? Sure. Happens all the time. By leaving your assets in a trust for your children, you can give them complete control over their inheritance (so you're not "ruling from the grave") while at the same time providing that, when they die, whatever they didn't spend goes to your grandchildren.

8. Guarantees you will be protected if you become disabled. An ever-increasing percentage of people today have a period of disability before they die. Without a plan, you risk getting the state's plan where they appoint a legal guardian for you who (1) may be a stranger (2) may change your investments (3) may be unable to protect your assets if you need long-term care, and (4) may make it difficult to get back control of your assets if you recover from your disability. When you set up a living trust, you avoid a guardianship

proceeding, put the persons you choose in control and allow them to transfer and protect assets, in order to qualify you for Medicaid benefits.

33

Leaving a Family Business

A farmer came in to see us with this dilemma. He had a working farm where his twenty something daughter and her husband were engaged full-time. His other daughter worked in the arts in New York City. He wanted to keep the farm in the family, but didn't know how.

He initially wanted to leave the farm and his other assets to the two daughters in equal shares. We cautioned against this since, we advised, no one likes to do all the work and then split the profits. Additionally, real estate prices could be considerably higher on his death and there might not be enough money in the estate for the working daughter to buy out her sister. We also had to consider the sweat equity the young couple would be building up over the years working the farm. Here's how the matter was ultimately resolved to the client's satisfaction.

We deeded the farm now to the working daughter (not her and her husband quite yet) reserving a "life estate" in the farmer so that he had a right to live there for the rest of his life and preserving his senior tax exemption on the property. We established the value of the property today, and made a bequest on his death, from the farmer's living trust, of a like amount in cash to the sister before the balance of the trust was divvied up.

Now the young working couple are secure in their future, the non-working daughter gets her fair share of the estate and the farmer is protected in his rights for life. Most important of all, he has the peace of mind in knowing that the farm will stay in the family.

If you're a business owner, and have one or more children working in the business, you have the same issues. We generally like to see the "working" children take over the business and other assets used to even out the estate distribution with the "non-working" children. Where there are not enough other assets to make the distribution even, then life insurance or a mortgage can be used for this purpose, or the "working" children can pay off the "non-working" children over a period of years at a rate the family business can afford.

34

Estate Planning for the Estranged Child

All too often a client comes in with a sad tale about an estranged child. Naturally, they are at a loss as to what to do about the situation when it comes to leaving that child an inheritance.

Years ago, the famous advice columnist Ann Landers wrote that her all time most requested column for reprint was on this very subject. Ann wrote that an inheritance should be considered a gift and that if the gift is not deserved one should not be expected. While that may have been good advice at the time and perhaps still is in most cases, like many things it is more complicated today.

In practice, we find that many of these once loving sons and daughters have married individuals with borderline or narcissistic personality disorders. Their spouses are manipulative and controlling. They seek to separate the loving son or daughter from their family so as to better control their spouse. The estranged child knows from experience that going against the wishes of their narcissistic spouse is like throwing gasoline on a fire -- so they go along to get along.

Why does this happen? The manipulator has an enormous advantage over the clients' son or daughter. The manipulator is a "professional", having been this way all their life, honing their skills. The estranged son or daughter is an amateur -- they have no experience in being manipulated. It may take years for them to even understand they are being manipulated and then more years, if ever, to build up defenses to the manipulation.

When young children are involved, the estranged child well knows the adverse consequences of having any normal relationship with their children should they seek a divorce from the narcissist.

Our advice is to try to understand and be compassionate with an estranged son or daughter in this situation. Set up an Inheritance Protection Trust (IPT) that may only be used for them and your grandchildren. The percentage to leave to, and who will be in charge of, the IPT is up to you.

Apart from having compassion for the estranged son or daughter married to the narcissist when considering leaving an inheritance, what about leaving an inheritance to the estranged child who is not in this situation.

The reasons for estrangement are as different as are families. As Tolstoy famously remarked, "Happy families are all alike; every unhappy family is unhappy in its own way".

One of the keys to resolving what to leave the estranged child is determining who in the family are they estranged from and for how long and for what reasons (if known). Sometimes they are estranged from only one parent and the other parent does not wish to see that child disinherited. Sometimes they are estranged from the parents but not their siblings -- or some but not all of their siblings. It's complicated. Often, hope springs eternal that the estranged son or daughter will come back into the fold.

In cases like these we like to use a technique we call "Schedule A". Generally, in a trust or a will, you will find the dispositive provisions, i.e. who you are leaving it to and in what amounts, somewhere in the middle of the document. When you amend the trust, or prepare a codicil to the will, you may legally change your wishes. Nevertheless, all of the parties can see what it was before and what the change was. For example, if you left someone out and now you are putting them back in, they will clearly see that they were left out before, and vice versa!

To avoid the hurt, confusion and possible litigation that these emotionally fraught situations may engender, we recommend using a "Schedule A" to the trust. Here, in the body of the trust we state that the wishes are provided in "Schedule A" annexed hereto which may be replaced from time to time with the same formalities as the execution of the trust. Now, when a change is made we destroy the old "Schedule A", replacing with the new one and avoiding hurt feelings and misunderstandings.

35

Don't Wait for Something to Happen to Start Planning

It is remarkable how many people fail to plan for the inevitable. Sooner or later, something happens to every person. About half of all people will eventually become disabled in the sense of being unable to handle their legal and financial affairs. Thankfully, for most of us it is later in life. But, unfortunately, not for all of us. Disability may strike at any time, regardless of age. Even if you are not part of the 50% who become disabled, the mortality rate is stubbornly stuck at 100%. Everyone needs a plan for death.

One day a client came in to see us about his mother who was hospitalized at age eighty-three from a car accident. Her husband, who should not have been driving according to the family, plowed into a parked car. His wife was not wearing a seat belt. She was hospitalized, breathing with the help of a ventilator and fed with feeding tubes. She could not get out of bed. Her son, the client, did not know if she knew who he was.

The son advised that he wanted to apply for Medicaid as his mother needed to go into a nursing home -- there was nothing more the hospital could do for her. When we inquired whether he wished for his mother to be kept alive in such an extreme state of disability, he said he was unaware of any other choice he had. We explained that if her health care proxy authorized it, he had the right to withdraw the feeding tubes whenever he felt it was the right time. He produced a health care proxy prepared by a relative -- it failed to authorize withdrawal of life support in extreme circumstances.

The client was left with the following situation. His mother never signed a power of attorney allowing someone to handle her legal and financial affairs. As a result he had to petition the court to be appointed her legal guardian in order to be able to apply for Medicaid benefits for her care. The whole process would take a number of stressful months, cost in the tens of thousands of dollars and there was no guarantee it would be successful. Don't wait for something to happen.

36

Celebrity Estate Planning Mishaps

Celebrity estate plans often involve extraordinary wealth. However, celebrities are still not immune to estate planning oversights and the consequences of poor planning.

When Robin Williams passed away, he had created an irrevocable trust to provide for his three children. One of the main reasons to create a trust is to protect your privacy. However, his trust documents were made public because one of the co-trustees he named passed away. The other trustee was forced to petition the court to appoint a successor co-trustee, because Mr. Williams had failed to name a successor.

Casey Kasem's final months created tabloid fodder of the conflict between his second wife and his children from his first marriage.

His wife challenged the court decision naming his daughter Kasem's guardian, and removed him from his nursing home to take control over his medical decisions. The dispute lasted for months over his medical care, and a lengthy court battle ensued after his death.

The lesson from Kasem's estate is to appoint in advance who will be in charge of your affairs if you are incapacitated, as well saying where your assets go on death.

One of Phillip Seymour Hoffman's greatest fears for his children was that they would grow up as entitled, trust fund kids. As a result, Hoffman gave his entire estate to his longtime girlfriend and mother of his children. Hoffman never created any trusts, never married, and his estate went through public probate. Had he married or set up trusts, his family would have avoided hefty estate taxes.

Michael Crichton earned millions from authoring popular novels, but he died unexpectedly while his fifth wife was pregnant with their child. Crichton never updated his estate plan to include his newest child. A court battle ensued between his last wife, representing their child, and his children from previous marriages.

The lesson from Crichton's estate is to update estate plans regularly as your life changes.

In his early eighties, the great comedic actor Tim Conway of The Carol Burnett Show fame, experienced significant cognitive decline. It was at this time that his daughter, Kelly Conway, who had a close relationship with her stepmom, Charlene, throughout the 34 years of her dad's second marriage, began an almost three year-long struggle with Charlene. Conflicts arose over whether to keep her father at home, which Conway wanted to protect her dad's privacy, or in a long-term care facility, which her stepmom ultimately chose.

As the conflict with her stepmom escalated when her father was moved to a new facility and Conway was barred from visiting, she enlisted the aid of an attorney to ensure she had visitation rights and access to the information on the care he was being provided. Through mediation, Conway was granted those legal visitation rights. However, her stepmother violated the order and continued to prohibit Conway from seeing her dad. Each visit required Conway getting her lawyer to call her stepmom's lawyer and insisting on her legal rights.

Grace Whiting, executive director of the National Academy of Elder Law Attorneys (NAELA), advises, "The goal of proper planning is for the individual's wishes to survive incapacity and to avoid the necessity of guardianship." But it can be hard to foresee the conflicts that can arise when a loved one is unable to speak on their own behalf. Since laws vary state to state and long-term care laws are complex, Whiting said an elder law attorney is fluent in these issues and can become a valuable resource for families.

On the day her father died, Kelly learned about it from a friend on the East Coast who heard it on the early news. There was no time left for her to fight for one last chance to see him and no phone call from her stepmom to advise of his passing.

Not wishing to let the story of one of America's greatest funny men end on a sad note, please search for Tim Conway's "The Dentist" on youtube.com to watch one of his very greatest (and funniest) skits.

37

Social Costs in Estate Planning

Everyone is concerned with financial costs but what about "social costs".

For example, trusts save money by avoiding court proceedings on death but what about saving time? Apart from the old saying that "time is money", there are social reasons for settling an estate quickly. Have you ever noticed that, after the will has been probated, brothers and sisters often never talk to each other again? Being tied up in a court proceeding over an estate is much like putting the children, not to mention the sons and daughters-in law, in business together. After all, there are often significant assets and everyone has a stake in the outcome. Some are in charge of the matter and some are not. Our view is that the sooner you can settle the estate, the more likely you will avoid the "social cost" of probate and the more likely it will be that your family stays together.

Quick settlement also aids in the grieving process, which can be delayed by the lack of closure involved in extended court proceedings.

Another social cost is the choice of asset distribution in the plan itself. Will the heirs be emotionally hurt or angry by how the estate is left? For example, a client without children, but with eleven nieces and nephews, recently proposed to leave her estate as follows: five thousand dollars to four of them, and the rest of her multi-million dollar estate in seven equal shares to the others. She had settled the estate of a sibling and received twenty thousand dollars in fees which she was "repaying" to the sibling's four children. The other seven were the ones she felt closest to.

We advised her to reconsider. The heirs who were getting the repayments might be left wondering why she waited decades to give the fees back, why she took the fees in the first place, or why they only got the original amount when it was worth so much more many years later. They might be hurt to learn that their cousins received much greater bequests. She decided that in the end leaving them out might save a considerable amount of ill will. Remember, how you leave your assets may result in hurt feelings that can last a lifetime.

38

Planning For and Executing Inheritances

Planning for, and then executing, inheritances is often fraught with emotion.

Most families choose to leave the inheritance "to my children in equal shares, per stirpes." Per stirpes is Latin meaning "by the roots" so that if a child dies before the parent, their share goes to their children (if any) in equal shares. If there are no children, then generally the inheritance is disregarded and their share goes to their surviving siblings in equal shares.

What about gifts to grandchildren? Let's say one child has five children and the other has two children -- seven grandchildren altogether. When a significant gift is given to grandchildren equally, it is not uncommon for the child with two children to say "well it was my brother's choice to have five children, why do I have to pay for it?" Good estate planning also looks at inheritances from the heirs' point of view as well.

We are often asked whether inheritances should be discussed with children ahead of time. While each family has different dynamics, this can end up being the equivalent of giving children a veto power over what you are going to do. For example, if you seek their opinion on an unequal division, you will create a problem for the family if you choose to disregard their input. A better way might be the use of the "soft probe". Here, you suggest an idea that you have about an unequal division, and then gauge their reaction before making a decision.

For example, where one child is very much better off than another, you might say "You know, your sister Mary could really use our money a lot more..." The monied child will generally respond one of two ways. They will either say "of course, I don't need it, leave it all to her" and you are off the hook, or they will indicate that they consider anything less than equal shares would be unfair. In the latter case, if you still want to help Mary more, you may give her gifts during your lifetime and keep peace in the family by leaving inheritances equally. You may also make some accounts joint with Mary or name her beneficiary and those accounts would not appear under the will or trust as part of the estate.

Early on, we learned the phrase "there's nothing so unequal as the equal treatment of unequals." Who has children that are all the same?

Some children have received significant help from parents during their lifetimes while others haven't. Many parents choose the "forgiveness provision" to address this situation at death, to either "equalize" any gifts made to some children during lifetime with those who did not receive gifts or, in the alternative, to "forgive" any loans made to children and then make a gift in like amount to each of the other children by inheritance, before the estate is divvied up in equal shares.

Next up is the problem of children who are partially or wholly estranged. Many clients wish to leave them a token amount but there are pitfalls to consider. One who is left considerably less than their siblings will often be angry and upset. They may demand that their siblings disclose what they received and even to pony up their equal share. Not only that, but the burden of telling that estranged child they are getting less and delivering the paltry amount is left to the children who you wish to favor!

In our view, it is sometimes better to leave an estranged child out altogether than to stir up all the issues surrounding an inheritance much smaller than equal.

There are many valid reasons, however, to treat children differently. They may have alcohol or substance abuse issues, learning disabilities or special needs, they may be immature and irresponsible, poor at handling money or a "soft touch" and, finally, they may have a spouse that dominates them and you do not want to see that controlling spouse get your money.

Sometimes parents leave more to the "needy" child, the old adage being that "the tongue always turns to the aching tooth". If so, other children's feelings may need to addressed. A letter to be opened after your death, explaining what you did and why, may go a long way towards soothing hurt feelings and avoiding misunderstandings.

39

Writing an Ethical Will

While a legal will bequeaths valuables, an ethical will bequeaths values, such as how to lead a moral and upright life. Questions of the heart and soul may creep in as we age – have I fulfilled my purpose? What will I be remembered for? What kind of legacy have I passed on to my family and others?

While not legally binding, ethical wills are excellent vehicles for clarifying and communicating the meaning of our lives to our families. Those who want to be remembered authentically and for their gifts of heart, mind and spirit, can take satisfaction in knowing what they hold most valued is "on the record," not to be lost or forgotten. Imagine the richness that might be added to our lives if we had a legacy such as this from our grandparents or our great-grandparents of whom many of us know little if anything at all.

When considering what you might include in your ethical will it may be productive to consider your past, present and future. Some of our values and beliefs have been passed on to us from our predecessors. Our own life experiences shape our character and help form a foundation of our values and principles. Looking into the future we might ponder what we may yet come to and what we have left to do.

An ethical will occurs in Hamlet when Polonius advises his son:

> "Give every man thy ear, but few thy voice,
> Take each man's censure, but reserve thy judgement...
> Neither a borrower not a lender (be),
> For (loan) oft loses both itself and friend...
> This above all: to thine own self be true,
> and it must follow, as the night the day,
> Thou canst not then be false of any man."

An ethical will is a forum in which to: (1) fill in knowledge gaps of heirs by providing historic or ancestral information that links generations (2) convey feelings, thoughts, and "truths", that are hard to say face-to-face (3) express regrets and apologies (4) open the door to forgiving and being forgiven, and (5) come to terms with our mortality.

40

Planning For Those You Are Responsible For

Once, a client came in to see us for their follow-up consultation. The client shared with us that, in between their two meetings with us, the husband's brother had suffered a stroke and was now in a rehabilitation facility. He was a bachelor. He had no power of attorney or health care proxy. He may or may not have had a will -- they didn't know. Further, they were unable to get access to his apartment to clean out the fridge and get his clothes because he had failed to put them on the list of persons approved to enter in the event of an emergency.

One of the most overlooked areas in estate planning is the question of who you are responsible for. Do you have a friend or relative who you know will need to rely on you if something happens?

Either they have no one else or everyone else is too far away. If you have the responsibility, then make sure that you have the documents you will need to carry out that responsibility. Otherwise, the challenges become of a magnitude greater.

Similarly, so many of our clients have adult children with young families. Do you know whether your children have wills, powers of attorney and health care proxies?

There are serious pitfalls for young families if one spouse dies without a plan. Roughly half of their assets go to their surviving spouse and half to the children. The court will appoint a legal guardian for the children's money and the unused portion must be turned over to them at age eighteen, ready or not!

A potentially more serious problem for older adults is whether their sons and daughters who have families possess adequate life insurance. If your son or daughter dies without sufficient life insurance, you may be called upon to support and educate your grandchildren out of your retirement money.

Finally, if you are responsible for the care of an elderly parent, then make sure it is you who has the power of attorney and health care proxy and not another sibling who may end up controlling the situation from afar, much to your dismay.

41

Leaving a Vacation Home to Family

We all know the road to you know where is paved with good intentions. Nowhere is this more true than leaving a vacation or beach home for the children to share after the parents have passed. We have often advised that if they are all happy and get along well this might very well lead to the end of those good feelings and relationships.

Inevitably, some will do more work on the premises than others, some will use the premises more than others, there will be disagreements as to maintenance and repairs. Some may never visit or use it at all.

Initially, all expenses tend to be shared equally, since all are equal owners. The foregoing issues, however, will quickly arise and then it will often be difficult or impossible to determine what each child's fair share of the expenses should be. The one living across the country who never visits may insist that they be "bought out" or, if that's unaffordable to the others, that the house be sold so that they can get their share.

Sooner or later, one of the siblings dies and their share goes to a sister-in-law or brother-in-law who may remarry and bring a stranger into the shared arrangement. Or let's say an owner of one-third of the house dies, and now their share goes to their four children. How is that going to work?

Vacation homes are an excellent example of why good estate planning is often more social work than legal work. In these cases we anticipate the problems and spend the time to figure out who wants and uses the home and perhaps leave it to those children only and compensate the others with money or other assets. If they all use and enjoy the home, we sometimes require that it be held jointly with the right of survivorship, allowing the last of the joint owners to decide who to leave it to.

42

Using "Moral Suasion" in Estate Planning

Attorneys are trained to create legally binding agreements. This approach may end up being heavy-handed when it comes to estate planning, often resulting in social problems for the family.

For example, lawyers will set up "inheritance trusts" to protect the inheritance from children's divorces, lawsuits and creditors and to keep the assets in the bloodline. To make these agreements legally binding, they will put two of the children in charge of the trust, requiring them to act together. This way the inheriting child cannot, for example, take assets out and give some to their spouse. Yes, it's legally binding but can be, and often is, a social disaster.

Let's say son wants to buy a condo in Florida. His sister thinks it's too expensive and doesn't agree. It's not hard to see what their relationship will be after that exchange! Similarly, when the parents have passed, often the children will say to each other "I don't want this, do you?" and will agree to "I'll give you yours if you give me mine" and then all of the trust protections are gone.

We believe there's a better way, based on the concept of "moral suasion". Moral suasion is an agreement based on argument and persuasion rather than coercion or legislation (Oxford). Ettinger Law Firm's proprietary "Inheritance Protection Trust" has the child acting as the sole trustee. The trust provides the protection from divorces, lawsuits and creditors, allows your son or daughter to use the funds for themselves and their children in equal or unequal amounts, and leaves it to the grandchildren at death. Yes, son or daughter can take all the money and give it to their spouse, but why would they? If this is any concern, such as their having a spouse that dominates them, then certainly you may name a co-trustee. In our experience, this occurs in only a tiny percentage of cases.

The advantages of using moral suasion are that it preserves the relationship between siblings and your son or daughter has no incentive to undo the trust, since they alone are in charge and may do whatever they wish with the assets.

With the high rate of divorce, along with an ever more litigious society, the Inheritance Protection Trust has become mainstream in estate planning today.

43

The Attorney-Client Relationship

Much can be said about the attorney-client relationship but mainly it is a relationship built on trust.

The client trusts that the attorney is knowledgeable and has the client's best interests at heart and, correspondingly, the client is respectful of the attorney's time and counsel. As Lincoln famously said, "A lawyer's time and advice are his stock in trade."

Some of the considerations in choosing an elder law estate planning firm should be:

- How long has the firm been in business
- How many attorneys does the firm employ

- Does the firm have a succession plan
- Does the firm review the plan regularly
- What do its clients say about the firm
- Does the firm charge for questions or emails
- How does the firm set its fees

While the client is interviewing the firm, the firm is also interviewing the client to see if there will be a good fit.

Seeing as we undertake to review your estate plan every three years, the plan is more than just a transaction. It is the beginning of a lifelong relationship between the law firm and your family. We will be sharing your trials and tribulations, offering experienced counsel when issues, sometimes difficult ones, arise all along the way. Often, we will also be advising your children as to the administration of the estate after you pass.

Relationship-wise, we strive to avoid negative relationships and situations as much as possible, allowing us to devote our full time and attention to the many fine and deserving clients we are privileged to serve.

At Ettinger Law Firm we are proud to have earned high Google ratings from a large number of clients (trustlaw.com). Considering the time and effort our attorneys and your family are putting in, a strong attorney-client relationship is essential.

44

The Privilege to Serve

A client recently thanked me for my patience in answering all of her questions, saying something to the effect that she knew she was a real pain. Quite to the contrary, I told her that it was a privilege to serve and thanked her for the opportunity.

We feel the same way about those we are privileged to have in our employ. We are fortunate to have them on our team. Everyone has choices and the choice to work for the benefit of our law firm is a decision we do not take lightly.

Perhaps it all comes down to generosity. Not just the giving of tangibles, but the giving of intangibles. The generosity of spirit. Who are the happiest amongst us? The givers, of course. And the more they give the happier they are. According to the Dalai Lama,

"We are self-centered and selfish, but we need to be wisely selfish, not foolishly so. If we neglect others, we too lose…we can educate people to understand that the best way to fulfill their own interests is to be concerned about the well-being of others."

There is no greater gift we can make than that of our time and attention. It is the most valuable resource each of us has to give -- since our time cannot be replenished, we are literally giving up our lives.

In "The Good Life", based on Harvard's 80 year scientific study of happiness, authors Robert Waldinger, MD and Marc Schultz, PhD, state "Time and attention are the essential materials of happiness. They are the reservoir from which our lives flow…so it never hurts to take a look at where our attention has been flowing, and ask if it's going into places that benefit both the people that we love and serve." The Harvard study concludes that the happiest and most satisfied adults were those who managed to turn the question "What can I do for myself?" into "What can I do for the world beyond me?"

Sometimes all it takes is the giving of your time and attention in the service of others to make you feel better about yourself.

45

Life Stories Preserved

As the title suggests, Life Stories Preserved is a service designed to preserve and perpetuate the lives and their meaning of people after they have left this good earth.

What prompted your author to share more about this service was the loss of my father recently at the age of ninety-one. I wrote and gave a fifteen minute or so eulogy. It didn't do justice to the man or his legacy. Not because it was inadequate, but because the vehicle, the eulogy, is inadequate to sum up a life so well lived such as his.

An old African proverb cited on the website, lifestoriespreserved.net says "When an elder dies, it is like a library has burned to the ground". How much richer would the lives of his grandchildren, great-grandchildren and so on, be had they known more about where they came from and what their forebearers have stood for and overcome. This author firmly believes ancestral stories can raise pride and self-esteem and make the lives of our loved ones, and of those in the future, deeper and more meaningful. Everybody wants to be someone from somewhere.

By interviewing family, friends, co-workers and business associates, this service weaves a tapestry of one's life in about twenty pages, often together with photos and documents. For the more ambitious, full-length books may be commissioned.

While these life stories are usually created during the subject's lifetime, they may also be done post-mortem. The focus may be as wide, such as a whole life, or as narrow as one would like, such as a period of one's life (for example, childhood) or a specific area (such as one's professional career).

Everyone has a fascinating story to tell but not everyone has the means, the inclination or the ability to tell it. The website states it succinctly "Sharing your or a loved one's life story and preserving family history and lore creates an invaluable legacy for future generations".

46

Donating Your Body to Science

As part of an elder law estate plan, many people include end of life directions, such as funeral and burial wishes, and possibly donating their bodies to science. Although most of the 170 medical schools across the country have implemented digital instruction into their anatomy labs, everyone still uses cadavers for instruction purposes.

However, donating your body for scientific research and education may be more difficult than it sounds. Some institutions require that you be within a certain driving distance or number of miles away. Others require a number of forms signed in advance by the donor, and not by a family member or even someone with a power of attorney.

The regulation of organ and body donation started in 1968 with the Uniform Anatomical Gift Act, which was adopted by all states and allows any individual to sign a "document of gift" that donates organs, tissue, or the full body for transplantation, therapy, research or education. Organ donation typically receives the most press, partially because of its dramatic life-saving miracles, but also because of the federal law that requires hospitals to refer families to the federal organ procurement organization (organdonor.gov).

If you wish to donate your body to science, arrangements must typically be made with a specific school. Each school creates its own policies regarding acceptance of donated bodies. Some schools have requirements beyond those of the Uniform Anatomical Gift Act regarding who can agree to donate, how far away the body can be, and certain details regarding the type of body that is acceptable.

In addition to completing all necessary paperwork with the chosen institution for donating your body, it is also very important to communicate with your loved ones to let them know of your plans and desires, including the location of the paperwork that may be needed when the time comes.

MEDICAID PLANNING STRATEGIES

47

Protecting Assets With Caregiver Agreements

Family members as caregivers overwhelmingly provide for elderly and disabled loved ones at home. Although a labor of love, taking care of ailing loved ones also has a market value, meaning that caretakers may be paid as a way to protect assets.

Through the use of a Caregiver Agreement, also known as a Personal Services Contract, the disabled or elderly person may transfer money to family members as compensation rather than as a gift. Gifts to family members made in the last five years before applying for Medicaid to pay for nursing home costs disqualify the applicant from receiving Medicaid for a certain period of time, known as a "penalty period."

For example, mom depends on daughter Janice for her care. If mom gifts $180,000 to Janice, then goes into a nursing home in the next five years and applies for Medicaid, the gift to Janice will result in about a ten month penalty period. Janice will have to give the $180,000 back to mom to pay nursing home costs during the penalty period, or mom will have to use other resources to pay.

Instead, using a Caregiver Agreement, mom pays Janice $3,000 per month for care giving services. If mom moves to the nursing home in five years, the $180,000 total payments to Janice are compensation, not gifts, and do not need to be paid back.

Caregiver Agreements must follow strict rules, so should be drafted by an experienced elder law attorney.

The Caregiver Agreement must detail the services to be performed and the obligations of the parties. The payment is based on the going rate of caretaking in that county. Compensation is clearly delineated with hourly and yearly calculations for 24-hour personal care.

Janice must actually give the care and document her caretaking duties. Mom must actually need the care, which should be documented with a doctor's note.

To protect family relationships, it's recommended that all family members agree with the arrangement even if they are not parties to the agreement.

Janice's compensation has tax consequences. She reports the payments as ordinary income on her income tax return and pays income taxes on the amount received. In some cases, mom may be able to deduct the payments as a medical expense.

A proper Caregiver Agreement arrangement may be a valuable elder law estate planning tool in the right circumstances.

48

Medicaid Asset Protection Trusts (MAPT)

Long-term care insurance is the preferred option for protecting assets from nursing home costs, since it helps keep clients out of the nursing home – by paying for home care. The trend today is to "age in place." Many clients over the years were forced to spend their final days in a facility simply because they ran out of money to pay for home health aides. Additionally, for married couples, the home care option may protect the spouse from compromising their own health and finances with the heavy burden of care giving in their later years. Too often, it is the caregiver spouse who dies first. We sometimes refer to the situation as a "perfect storm". The spouse caregiver is often in their eighties or nineties, the job is 24/7/365 and it is a very hard one.

When the client is turned down for long-term care insurance, or is unable to afford the premium, the next best option is the Medicaid Asset Protection Trust (MAPT). Making assets joint with adult children offers no protection since Medicaid considers all of the jointly held assets to be available for the care of the ill parent, except to the extent the child can prove the amount of their actual contribution. Additionally, outright transfers to children are generally inadvisable since those assets then become exposed to the child's debts and liabilities, divorces, etc. In addition, some children spend the money, refuse to give it back when needed or die before the parent and pass those assets on to their heirs. One exception to the inadvisability of outright transfers to children is when long-term care is imminent or at least foreseeable. In such a case, the assistance of an elder law attorney is essential since the amounts to be transferred, the order of assets transferred and where to transfer the assets all require the advice of counsel. The object here would be to protect as much of the assets as possible and to qualify for Medicaid benefits at the earliest possible moment. If someone is just getting older, can't or won't get long-term care insurance and wants to plan ahead to protect their assets, the best option is to create a Medicaid Asset Protection Trust (MAPT).

Known as an irrevocable "income only" trust, the MAPT names someone other than you or your spouse as the trustee, usually one or more adult children, and limits you to the income. The principal must be unavailable in order for it to be protected. These trusts are ideal for the family home as well as for assets the client is only taking the income from or is simply reinvesting. The client's lifestyle is not generally affected since they continue to receive their pension and Social Security checks directly, they keep the

Medicaid Planning Strategies

exclusive right to use and occupy the home and they preserve all the property tax exemptions on the home. The trust may sell and trade assets through the trustee. Nevertheless, the parent retains some measure of control by reserving the right to change the trustee in the event of dissatisfaction for any reason.

Transfers to the MAPT are subject to a look-back period of up to five years for facility care and potentially a new two and a half year look-back period for home care services. This means, for example that if assets are transferred to the MAPT, and the client needs nursing home care any time after five years have passed, the assets in the trust are protected. Nevertheless, it always pays to get started, since you get credit for the time you accumulate, even if you don't make the five years. For example, if the client needs nursing home care, say, after only four years, then they would only have to pay for the one year that's left on the look-back.

The Medicaid Asset Protection Trust is also flexible. You may sell the home, the money is paid to the trust, and the trust may buy a condominium, for example. The condo is still protected since it is owned by the trust and the five year look back does not start over since nothing was transferred from you to the trust. The trust simply sold one asset and purchased another, as it is permitted to do.

The trust may buy, sell and trade stocks and other assets. IRA's and other qualified plans stay out of the trust since the principal of all such retirement plans are exempt from Medicaid. These types of assets also avoid probate as they go directly to the designated beneficiaries at death.

Medicaid Planning Strategies 172

The MAPT is called "irrevocable" because you, the grantor, may not revoke it yourself. However, in New York we may still revoke the MAPT provided all the named parties agree in writing. Since this is most often just you and your immediate family, it is generally not difficult to revoke an "irrevocable" trust.

MAPT v. Life Estate Deed

Clients often ask whether the home should be deeded to the client's adult children, while retaining a life estate in the parent or whether the Medicaid Asset Protection Trust should be used to protect the asset.

While the deed with a life estate will be less costly to the client, in most cases it offers significant disadvantages when compared to the trust. First, if the home is sold prior to the death of the Medicaid recipient, the life estate value of the home will be required to be paid towards their care. If the house is rented, the net rents are payable towards their care since they belong to the life tenant. Finally, the client loses a significant portion of their capital gains tax exclusion for the sale of their primary residence as they will only be entitled to a pro rata share based on the value of the life estate to the home as a whole. All of the foregoing may lead to a situation where the family finds they must maintain a vacant home for many years. Conversely, a properly drafted MAPT preserves the full capital gains tax exclusion on the sale of the primary residence and the home may be sold by the trust without obligation to make payment of any of the principal towards the client's care, assuming we have passed the look-back period.

It should be noted here that both the life estate and the irrevocable Medicaid trust will preserve the stepped-up basis in the property provided it is only sold after the death of the parent who was the owner or grantor. Upon the death of the parent, the basis for calculating the capital gains tax is stepped up from what the parent paid, plus any improvements, to what it was worth on the parent's date of death. This effectively eliminates payment of capital gains taxes on the sale of appreciated property, such as the home, after the parent dies.

MAPT Do's and Don'ts

The following is a convenient list of "Do's and Don'ts" in managing the MAPT.

Do's

- Do make all transfers to your trust, as advised by the elder law firm, in a timely manner.

- Do take dividends and income on trust assets on at least a quarterly basis (if not, they are considered additions to principal and create a new look-back on the money not taken every year).

- Do contact the elder law firm when you wish to make a gift from the trust to any of your beneficiaries.

- Do contact the elder law firm when a grantor needs Medicaid benefits or dies.

- Do contact the elder law firm when personal or financial circumstances change significantly.

- Do contact the elder law firm if you wish to change trustees or undo the trust.

- Do provide your homeowner's insurance company with a "letter of instruction", including a copy of the trust for real property transferred to the trust, to add the trustees as "additional insureds" (supplied by the law firm).

- Do provide your CPA or tax preparer with a "letter of instruction" regarding the trust tax return (supplied by the law firm).

- Do choose your trustee carefully to avoid the expense (and unpleasantness) of having to change the trustee.

- Do contact the elder law firm if you want to refinance, take a reverse mortgage or take out a home equity line of credit ("HELOC") on real property in the trust.

Don'ts

- Don't use trust assets to pay telephone or utility bills.

- Don't use trust assets to pay personal expenses.

- Don't use trust assets to purchase an automobile (since all the assets in the trust will be exposed to liability if there is a car accident).

- Don't take principal or capital gains from trust assets.

- Don't transfer IRA's or 401(k)'s to the trust.

- Don't allow beneficiaries to return to the trust or the grantor any gifts made from trust assets.

- Don't make additional transfers to the trust in the future without advising the elder law estate planning firm.

- Don't use trust assets for repairs and improvements on grantor's residence (permitted for rental property).

- Don't use trust assets for payment of real estate taxes and homeowner's insurance on grantor's residence (permitted for rental property).

49

Seven Myths About MAPT's

Over the years I have been asked this question many times – "Why don't more people do the Irrevocable Medicaid Asset Protection Trust (MAPT)?" Well, actually, many people do.

For those who don't, the answer is simple – clients often receive incorrect advice on elder law from well meaning but ill informed advisors -- accountants, financial planners, general practice lawyers or others.

Here are seven myths clients have come in to see us with due to incorrect advice.

Myth #1: When you put your house into the MAPT you can't sell it.

I actually had a divorce lawyer representing my client's soon to be ex-husband insist that she could not sell her house in the MAPT. I wrote back that this was nonsense, having done it many hundreds of times and advising that nothing in the trust prohibits the sale. The proceeds are payable to the trust and remain protected. The trust may then buy a condo for example and the look-back period does not start over.

Myth #2: You lose your Senior, Veteran's and STAR exemptions.

Not correct. A properly drafted MAPT preserves all of the homeowner's property tax exemptions as well as the exemption from capital gains tax on the sale of the primary residence -- $500,000 for a couple or $250,000 for a single person.

Myth #3: You have to wait five years.

While it is true that it takes five years to protect all of the assets in the MAPT, many are unaware the time "pro rates". For example, if the client has to go into the nursing home after four years have passed they only have to pay for the one year that is left.

Myth #4: You can't change the trustee.

You've been around, you know things happen, so you reserve the right to change the trustee at any time. Not only does this keep them honest but it gives you control. Your son or daughter may be in charge of the trust – but you are in charge of them.

Myth #5: You can't change who you leave it to.

Similar to #4 above, in a well-drafted MAPT you reserve the right to change who you leave it to – knowing that sometimes wishes change.

Myth #6: You can only get income from the trust.

While it is true that you can only get income from the trust it does not mean you have no use of the principal. You retain the right to make gifts of principal in any amount to any of your children.

Myth #7: You cannot revoke the MAPT.

Strange as it may seem, in New York you may revoke an irrevocable trust. Here's why. It's irrevocable because you, the grantor, cannot revoke it alone. So as far as you're concerned, it's an irrevocable trust. However, New York has another rule on the books that says that if every person named in the irrevocable trust agrees in writing that they no longer want the trust, then you may revoke it on consent of all the named parties. Since that is just you and your adult children, it is usually a simple matter to accomplish. One of the reasons for a revocation might be the client has chosen to live in a life-care community that includes nursing home care as part of the buy-in.

50

Home Care With Community Medicaid

To qualify for community based Medicaid, meaning receiving medical care in the home, an individual cannot make more than $1,677 per month and a married couple cannot make more than $2,268 per month. Obviously, these minimal income standards make it very difficult to qualify for community Medicaid. However, applicants can "spend down" excess income to meet the Medicaid income requirement.

Also, an individual cannot own more than $30,182 in assets and a married couple cannot own more than $40,821 in assets.

There are two ways to spend down income. First, the applicant can reduce the income by paying for caregiving and other medical expenses. Second, the income can be reduced through the use of a "pooled income trust" where participants deposit their funds in a general trust, each with their own sub-account within the pooled trust.

A pooled trust, which is available in all states, must be run by a non-profit organization, and exists for elderly and disabled individuals for the purpose of supplementing the participants' needs beyond government benefits. In the case of people who may not qualify for community Medicaid because of excess income, the pooled trust can allow them to stay at home, also known as "aging in place."

"Special" or "supplemental needs" trusts may also be established through a pooled trust for disabled individuals under age 65 but the focus of this chapter is the use of the "pooled income trust" to keep people at home who need long-term care if their income exceeds required levels.

For example, Ralph applies for community Medicaid to allow him to stay at home and have home health aids, paid by Medicaid, to come in to assist in his care. His monthly income is $4,000, and he doesn't have excess medical costs to spend-down. He can deduct his Medicare Part B premium, his private insurance premium and $20 of income. For this purpose, we'll estimate total deductions of $300, leaving a countable net income of $3,700. From this amount, you deduct the $1,677 he's allowed, which results in a spend-down of $2,023.

When Ralph joins the pooled trust, he sends his spend-down amount of $2,023 to the pooled trust administrator every month. Each month, he submits to the administrator non-medical bills in his name for rent, mortgage, telephone, utilities, cable, life insurance, auto insurance, and the like. The trust pays those bills directly up to the amount he contributed. Ralph does not receive any cash. Medicaid pays for his home care on a level determined necessary by Medicaid, based on Ralph's medical needs. Assuming he is otherwise eligible for Medicaid, Ralph qualifies for community Medicaid despite his income level.

Several non-profit organizations exist that offer pooled trusts. Applying to join a pooled trust is a formal process. Costs generally include minimal start-up fees, an initial deposit and reasonable maintenance fees. Upon the death of the participant, that individual's remaining balance stays in the pooled trust to benefit other participants.

51

Long-Term Care Insurance v. MAPT

Long-term care insurance (LTCI) and the Medicaid Asset Protection Trust (MAPT) are often thought of as alternatives to each other. They are not. While LTCI is both a shield and a sword, the MAPT is a shield only.

LTCI protects your assets and income from the costs of care. But it has a positive effect (the sword) in that it actually pays for someone to come into your home and care for you there. The MAPT protects assets, like your home and your life savings, but it does not protect your income (pensions, social security, interest, dividends, etc.). The MAPT is solely a defensive tactic. That being said, in the event LTCI is unavailable to the client for medical or financial reasons, the MAPT is an excellent tool. There is truth in the saying that a good defense is the best offense. With the MAPT in place five years ahead of time, the client's assets are protected and Medicaid will then pay for the cost of care. While income may be protected for community care in the home, with the pooled income trust (Chapter 50), for institutionalized care in a facility your income is available to pay towards your care. If you have a spouse at home, they may keep about $3,435 per month of the couple's combined income and sometimes more, depending on whose income it is -- the community spouse's or the institutionalized spouse's.

Our stated preference for clients is LTCI, if available. Most clients would prefer to "age in place" or, in other words, stay in their own home and receive home care if needed. Here, the LTCI stretches your dollars to allow you to remain in the home for years more than you might have been able to afford otherwise. If your spouse is unable to care for themselves, it allows you to call in extra help so that you do not wear yourself out acting as a caregiver in your later years. Unfortunately, studies show that spouse caregivers often die first due to the stress of care giving.

Some clients have adopted a hybrid approach when it comes to LTCI and the MAPT. They purposely underfund the LTCI, say taking a $300/day benefit ($9,000/month) instead of a $600/day benefit ($18,000/month). They also establish the MAPT and transfer their assets to the trust. The thinking is that the $300/day will pay for the home care that they may need and want, at half the cost of the full policy. On the other hand, if they end up in a nursing home, they won't lose their assets due to the $9,000/month they may be short, and Medicaid will pick up the difference.

52

Applying for Medicaid

In the event the client requires home care or institutionalized care in a nursing home facility, an application for Medicaid benefits may be required. Due to complex asset and transfer rules, the application should be made with the aid of an experienced elder law attorney. Again, it is useful in this context for a confidential survey of the client's assets, as well as any transfers of those assets, to be filled out prior to the initial consultation. This form of financial survey will be significantly different from the one used for estate planning purposes. As a combined federal and state program, Medicaid asset and transfer rules vary significantly from state to state.

There are two different kinds of Medicaid, Community Medicaid and Chronic Care Medicaid.

Community Medicaid

Community based Medicaid applications are for any elderly/disabled person who wishes to remain in the community, in the setting of their own home. This benefit requires three (3) months of financial documentation, current proof of income, along with "common documents" and the past year's income tax filing, with 1099's. New rules will gradually extend the look-back period to two and a half years, thus requiring thirty (30) months of financial documents.

Although only low income recipients may qualify for this benefit, any middle income person may qualify for this benefit by using the pooled income trust to shelter excess income. By using the pooled income trust even middle class people may become eligible for community Medicaid.

Once benefits have been applied for and a Medicaid "pick-up" date has been established, the applicant may keep some of their monthly income and the balance is required to be contributed to their care, unless sheltered with the pooled income trust. The amounts you may retain are constantly changing and are naturally different for singles and couples. Consult with an elder law attorney for the going rates in your community at any given time.

Resources, which are assets belonging to the applicant and/or community spouse, must be reported and an individual is allowed to keep only a modest amount, around $30,000. If there is a spouse at home, the resource allowance may be as much as $150,000.

Chronic Care

Perhaps your loved one may no longer stay at home because they have become a danger to themselves or others. Maybe they need too much care or their caregiver is no longer able to manage their care. In such a case you may want to apply for chronic care benefits.

The Chronic Care application requires a look-back of five years, or sixty months. You must provide all financial statements of any open or closed accounts in this time period. Each county is different in the type of documentation you will need to present. Again, all "common documents" must be presented, five years of tax returns, proof of income, and the correct application.

The Department of Social Services will look for any gifts or transfers made in the look-back period (gifts to children, friends, grandchildren, church donations, charitable donations, etc.). Each gift will incur a penalty period determined by the state Medicaid Regional Rates chart published each year. Should you apply before the penalty period has expired you may be asked to provide additional documentation.

On all applications the county will begin an investigation. They will request an IRS report for the past five years, they will request a DMV report to see what vehicles are or were owned, they will request a financial institution report under the applicant's and his/her spouse's Social Security number and if something has not been reported the department may charge the applicant with fraud if they feel a deliberate attempt was made to hide assets.

Medicaid Planning Strategies

In our experience, most individuals who attempt to file for Medicaid benefits, without the assistance of counsel, either complete the application incorrectly, do not provide the correct documentation or give unnecessary information which causes the county to investigate further. These types of errors may require an appeal, known as a Fair Hearing, to have the matter rectified.

An individual applying for chronic care benefits and who is in a nursing home is required to pay virtually all of their income towards their care. The community spouse, if there is one, is allowed to keep about $3,700 per month in income and, if they fall short, the institutionalized spouse is allowed to contribute some of their income to the community spouse before paying the nursing home.

53

Medicaid Exempt Assets

Under Medicaid, the combined assets of spouses are available for the care of the ill or "institutionalized" spouse, regardless whose name those assets are in.

Nevertheless, many assets or "resources" are exempt from Medicaid when there is a spouse at home (the "community spouse"). These are:

- The home up to a value of $1,033,000

- $74,820 to $146,620 in resources

- One automobile

- Prepaid funeral and burial for applicant and spouse

- Household furniture, personal effects, jewelry with sentimental value

- IRA's, 401(k)'s and other qualified plans, provided they are paying out a monthly income

- Annuities paying out a monthly income naming spouse as primary beneficiary

- Medicaid Asset Protection Trust (MAPT) assets, if held in trust more than five years for facility care and two and a half years for home care

- Assets in trusts set up by someone other than the applicant (or their spouse)

- Supplemental Needs Trusts (also known as "Special Needs Trusts") for the benefit of a disabled person under age sixty-five

- Pooled income trusts for disabled persons subject to county approval

The above exemptions create some planning opportunities. Should the Medicaid applicant have a disabled child or grandchild, they can immediately protect any assets they choose to place into a Special Needs Trust (SNT) for the child or grandchild (Chapter 7).

Medicaid Planning Strategies

Since the home is an exempt asset when a spouse is living there, so are repairs and improvements to the home, including new carpeting, appliances, kitchen, baths, modifications for handicapped accessibility, lifts for stairs, etc. A mortgage can be paid off to reduce the amount of assets required to be "spent down" in order to obtain Medicaid eligibility. Although only one automobile is allowed, nothing prevents the spouse from trading in the old clunker for a brand new car.

When there is no spouse, the resource allowance falls to about $30,000. The home and automobile, no longer needed by the applicant, are no longer exempt. Nevertheless, the home may still be protected if an adult child was living in the home and caring for the parent for the two year period immediately prior to the parent entering the nursing home under the "primary caregiver" rule. Care in this context is interpreted broadly. The home may also be protected if a sibling of the applicant lived in the home for at least one year and has an "equity interest", the latter term also being broadly interpreted. All of the other exemptions listed above, if there is a spouse, also apply if there is no spouse.

Income exemptions also depend on whether or not there is a spouse. For nursing home care, the community spouse may keep about three thousand seven hundred dollars per month of the couple's income. In the case where the spouse's income exceeds the threshold, the spouse may keep most of his or her own excess income as well. The rules also allow keeping greater "resources" to generate the income necessary to meet the exemption, if the income is not otherwise available, although this must be applied for. Veterans' "Aid and Attendance" benefits are also exempt.

Medicaid Planning Strategies

Clients often ask whether Medicaid can "go after" the assets when the community spouse dies after the institutionalized spouse. If the assets were exempt, then Medicaid has no "right of recovery" since Medicaid was properly paid. However, if assets are left by will to a surviving institutionalized spouse, Medicaid will assert a claim. If the assets were left to someone other than the spouse, Medicaid may seek to exercise the institutionalized spouse's "right of election" since spouses are entitled to claim a share of the estate if they are disinherited. Proper planning with an elder law attorney can avoid these unfortunate results.

54

Medicaid Annuities to Protect Assets

Medicaid annuities have been a viable planning option for spouses since The Deficit Reduction Act of 2005.

Say you have a spouse who needs nursing home care (the "institutionalized spouse") but you have more assets than the Medicaid law allows you, the spouse at home (the "community spouse") keep. Currently, the community spouse may keep up to about $150,000 in resources (not including the house, which is exempt if a spouse is living there up to about $1,000,000 in equity). But what if the couple has $400,000 in assets? That's $250,000 in excess resources.

Many well meaning advisers, including lawyers, will tell you that it is too late and you have to first spend down that $250,000 before

Medicaid will pay. This is incorrect advice.

Elder law attorneys have a number of good planning options here, such as "spousal refusal" and the "gift and loan" strategy, discussed in subsequent chapters. Another planning option, the Medicaid annuity, may in some cases turn out to be the best planning option.

The community spouse purchases a Medicaid annuity worth the excess $250,000, which annuity must make repayments of the full amount of the annuity plus interest within the community spouse's actuarial life expectancy. Now, the $250,000 has disappeared and the institutionalized spouse is immediately eligible for Medicaid, saving nursing home costs of sometimes $18,000 or more per month. Spouse at home also receives an increased income which is also almost all sheltered from Medicaid.

55

Spousal Refusal – "Just Say No"

Spousal refusal is a legally valid Medicaid planning option in just two states: New York and Florida. By way of background, certain income and assets are exempt from Medicaid if there is a spouse. Generally, the spouse at home, known as the "community spouse" may keep about $3,700 per month of the couple's combined income and up to about $150,000 of the assets or "resources". Not included in those figures are any other exempt assets, such as a home and one automobile. The spouse who is being cared for in a facility is known as the "institutionalized spouse".

Many a spouse has advised us that they simply cannot afford to live on the allowances that Medicaid provides. This is where spousal refusal comes in. We start by shifting excess assets into the name of the community spouse. He or she then signs a document which the elder law attorney prepares and files with the Department of Social Services indicating that they refuse to contribute their income and assets to the care of the ill spouse since they need those income and assets for their own care and well-being. Note that you may not refuse your spouse's own income over the $3,700 per month exemption as it is not coming to you.

Once the community spouse invokes their right to refuse, and all of the other myriad requirements of the Medicaid application are met, the state Medicaid program must pay for the care of the institutionalized spouse.

After Medicaid has been granted, the county may institute a lawsuit seeking to recover the cost of care from the refusing spouse. Nevertheless, there are a few reasons why spousal refusal makes sense, even in light of this risk. First, in many instances, the county never invokes this right. Secondly, these lawsuits are often settled for significantly less than the cost of care provided. Thirdly, the payment to the county can sometimes be deferred until the community spouse dies. As one county attorney told us when agreeing to such an arrangement, "the county is going to be around for a long time". Finally, even though the county may seek recovery, it is only for the Medicaid reimbursement rate and not the private pay rate. For example, if the private pay rate is $18,000 per month, which is what you would have to pay, the amount Medicaid has to pay is much less in most cases. So the Medicaid rate at the same facility may be only $12,000 per month. The county may only pursue you for the amount they actually paid. Worst case scenario then, if you had to repay the county, is that you would still be saving $6,000 per month for the cost of your spouse's care.

Medicaid Planning Strategies

Spousal refusal is an excellent option for spouses who find one of them on the nursing home doorstep. Far better, however, is to plan ahead with long-term care insurance or, where such insurance is not available for medical or financial reasons, consider setting up a Medicaid Asset Protection Trust (MAPT) at least five years ahead of time to protect your home and life savings.

56

Saving Half on the Nursing Home Doorstep

What do you do when a client comes in to see you and says that his mother is going into a nursing home and she has $360,000 in assets. In fact, mom scrimped and saved all of her life to have this nest egg and now she desperately wants to see her children get an inheritance.

Although you may protect all of your assets by planning five years ahead of time with a Medicaid Asset Protection Trust, all is not lost if nothing has been done and the client finds herself on the nursing home doorstep.

The advanced elder law technique, used to protect assets at the last minute, is called the "gift and loan" strategy. Here's how it works. Let's assume, for the purposes of our example, that the nursing home costs $18,000 a month. When mom goes into the nursing home, we gift one-half of the nest egg, in this case one-half of $360,000, or $180,000, to her children. Then we lend the other $180,000 to the children and they execute a promissory note agreeing to repay the $180,000 in ten monthly payments of $18,000 per month, together with a modest amount of interest. Now we apply for Medicaid benefits. Medicaid will impose a penalty period (i.e., they will refuse to pay) for 10 months on the grounds that the gift of $180,000 could have been used to pay for mom's care for 10 months. Medicaid ignores the loan since it was not a gift. It is going to be paid back, with interest, according to the terms of the promissory note. What happens is that the ten loan repayment installments will be used to pay for mom's nursing home care during the penalty period. Just when the loan repayments are finished, the penalty period expires and Medicaid begins to pick up the tab. Lo and behold, the children get to keep the $180,000 gift and mom has saved some of the inheritance for her children.

Also known as "half-a-loaf planning", this technique has been approved in most states. And, of course, everyone knows what half-a-loaf is better than, right?

ESTATE ADMINISTRATION UPON DEATH

57

Estate Administration and Probate

Probate is the legal proceeding in which the probate court assumes jurisdiction over the assets of someone who has died. The court supervises the payment of debts, taxes, and probate fees, and then supervises the distribution of the remainder to the persons named in a will, or to the legal heirs if there is no will. Probate may not be necessary if a deceased person had a properly drafted and funded trust. However, trust administration is necessary.

Family members commonly believe that their deceased loved one properly planned because the decedent had a will, had created and funded a trust, or had designated certain individuals as beneficiaries. In fact, sometimes the decedent's plans may actually have a negative impact on the family with regard to estate taxes, and/or Medicaid planning strategies for the surviving spouse. If this occurs, experienced elder law estate planning attorneys can advise you about post-mortem planning techniques that may rectify the situation and create more favorable tax consequences for surviving family members. Assets that were "exempt" for Medicaid while the spouse was living may now be "available", such as the home. It is always a good idea to review the estate plan after the first spouse dies.

Unlike a will, a trust is a private document and need not be filed with the probate court on death. Nonetheless, the successor trustee must still take steps to administer the trust: beneficiaries must be contacted and kept informed; the grantor's assets gathered and invested; any debts paid; potential creditors notified; taxes filed and paid; assets and/or income distributed in conformity with trust provisions to beneficiaries, etc.

Successor trustees often lack the time, resources or knowledge to personally administer the trust, and therefore may call upon legal, accounting and investment professionals for assistance.

Successor Trustee's Obligations

Below is a summary of the basic obligations of a successor trustee of a trust.

Show loyalty to all trust beneficiaries. Even if the successor trustee is himself a beneficiary, as trustee he has the duty of loyalty to all the other beneficiaries, including the contingent beneficiaries.

Deal impartially with beneficiaries. The successor trustee may not favor the lifetime income beneficiary over the interests of the remainder beneficiaries who will take after the death of the lifetime beneficiary. Investments must balance the need for income with the requirement for growth to offset inflation.

Make the trust property productive of income. This duty is violated if the successor trustee keeps large amounts in a checking account that does not pay interest and does not grow in value. There may be other trust assets which do not produce income, such as a vacant home. These assets must be disposed of or made productive within a reasonable time, since they are considered "wasting" assets which deplete the estate. The trustee may be liable for failing to convert "wasting" assets into productive assets.

Invest only in prudent investments. The prudent investor rule requires:

- Consideration by the trustee of the purposes, terms and other circumstances of the trust.

- Exercise reasonable care and caution as part of an overall investment strategy which incorporates risk and return objectives reasonably suitable to the trust.

- Diversity of investments, unless specific reasons are present not to diversify.

- Review and implementation of a formal investment plan.

- An investment strategy that considers both the reasonable production of income and safety of principal, consistent with the fiduciary's duty of impartiality towards the beneficiaries and the purposes of the trust.

Account to beneficiaries and keep beneficiaries informed. Upon commencement of the trust administration, the successor trustee must inform all income and remainder beneficiaries of their acceptance of the trust. If a beneficiary requests it, the successor trustee is required to provide that beneficiary with a complete copy of the trust document, including any amendments as well as relevant information about the assets of the trust and the particulars relating to administration. In addition, all beneficiaries must be provided with an annual statement of the accounts of the trust upon request.

Keep trust assets separate. The successor trustee must keep the assets of each trust separate and keep his personal assets separate from the trust assets. This requires separate bank accounts, brokerage accounts, and safe deposit boxes for trust assets. It is particularly important that you keep the assets of the deceased spouse's Credit Shelter Trust (also known as the AB Trust or Bypass Trust), if they had one, separate from all other assets, since these assets will pass tax-free at the death of the surviving spouse. If the surviving spouse, acting as trustee, commingles any other assets in with these assets (or even simply takes the assets out of the trust and mixes them with their personal assets), in addition to breaching fiduciary obligations, the successor trustee will have subjected these otherwise exempt assets to taxation when they die.

Avoid conflicts of interest and self dealing. The successor trustee cannot buy assets from the trust or sell his personal assets to the trust. He cannot favor himself as a beneficiary at the expense of any other remainder or potential remainder beneficiary. He cannot make any distribution to anyone or any withdrawals from the trust unless specifically authorized by the trust to do so. Conflicts of interest and self-dealing are often vague and ill-defined. If you are a trustee and have any concern as to any specific action or situation, consult with an experienced attorney.

Preserve the trust assets and uphold the trust. The successor trustee is liable if trust assets are lost, misplaced or destroyed because of inattention or negligence. The successor trustee should always be certain that all trust assets are appropriately protected and insured.

File tax returns and pay any tax due. Each trust has a tax year, which like the personal tax year, ends annually on December 31. The trust must have a taxpayer identification number and file a tax return no later than April 15 of the year following. The income tax return for the trust is Form 1041, the Fiduciary Income Tax Return. If this is not filed annually and timely, penalties and interest may be assessed. There may be other tax returns and taxes, like the decedent's personal tax return, which the trust may be required to file, and the successor trustee is responsible for doing so.

We recommend that successor trustees consult with a qualified and experienced certified public accountant. You should not assume that your long-time CPA is necessarily experienced or qualified, since fiduciary taxation differs significantly from taxation of individuals and corporations, the types of accounting that CPA's are generally most familiar with. Before deciding on a CPA for the trust, determine whether that individual has experience and qualifications in this specialized area.

Distribute income. Income generally includes interest earned on bank accounts, CD's, bonds or mortgages, and dividends on stocks and mutual funds. The current income beneficiaries are entitled to all of the income annually. Beneficiaries cannot choose to take less than all of the income, and the trustee is under an obligation to distribute it. Certain types of income may also consist of principal as well as income. If this is the case, the portion that is income is distributed and the portion that is principal is retained. If there is any question about what is principal and what is income, consult with the trust's CPA.

Handle trust expenses. The administration of the trust necessarily requires certain expenditures. Example of expenses include CPA fees, legal services, the cost of insurance or real estate taxes on real estate owned by the trust. Every check written by the successor trustee (except to pay trust income) and each direct charge to a trust's bank or brokerage account, is considered a trust expense. Like receipts, expenses must also be appropriately apportioned between the income side and the principal side.

Delegate investment functions if necessary. In many instances, individual trustees are not equipped to comply with their investment responsibilities. In these cases, investment professionals may be retained. The successor trustee is obligated to exercise reasonable care, judgment and caution in selecting an investment agent. Trust administration specialists may be found through brokerage houses, banks and some law firms. Note that "delegating" differs from merely obtaining investment advice. It contemplates turning over the investment functions to an advisor as opposed to simply seeking advice, and then acting or not acting on that advice. Even if investment functions are fully turned over to an agent, the successor trustee is still required to monitor the agent's investment performance.

A successor trustee should not assume that he has satisfied his investment responsibilities just because he has consulted regularly or occasionally with a stockbroker. Further, stockbrokers are often unaware of the prudent investor rule and fiduciary duties of a successor trustee.

Good record keeping. Keeping accurate, up-to-date and comprehensive records is one of the most difficult jobs a successor trustee must perform. If the successor trustee becomes disabled or dies, another person must be able to seamlessly step into his shoes and understand the current status of trust matters. Trust records are also vital because the trustee must be able to explain any trust matter if the IRS or remainder beneficiary requests it. The CPA selected to handle the trust can be very helpful in setting up a sound accounting and record-keeping system. If keeping records is too burdensome for the successor trustee, he can retain the trust department of a bank, the CPA or the law firm to do the work on a fee basis.

58

Trustee's Duties Upon Death

Here's a "to do" list, including both legal and practical responsibilities, of the trustee upon the death of the grantor.

• Locate and review all of the deceased's important papers. Sometimes directions for funeral and other pertinent information may be located in the deceased's papers, so these documents should be reviewed as quickly as possible.

• If the deceased was living alone, change locks and take any steps necessary to close the house or other residence. If the house will be vacant, insurance carriers should be notified of this fact. Check on auto and property insurance to be certain trust assets are insured against loss or liability.

- Obtain at least six certified copies of the death certificate from the funeral director, or the city, town or village clerk where the death occurred.

- Make a list of all household goods to be distributed to beneficiaries. To be absolutely safe, if several beneficiaries are involved, photograph personal property and take an unrelated, disinterested witness along when you make your list.

- Create a complete list of all assets and establish the value of those assets. The value at the time of death determines the new tax basis of appreciated assets, since all capital gains on assets is forgiven upon death. Even if the real estate, stock, or any other appreciated asset is not sold immediately, establishing a fair market value as of date of death is necessary to establish the new tax basis for future appreciation purposes, to determine whether state or federal estate tax is an issue, and to equitably distribute assets to beneficiaries as provided in the trust agreement.

- If several different accounts exist, it simplifies things greatly if liquid assets are consolidated into one account (or one savings and one checking account). That way, the check register for the account becomes a record of bills paid, deposits made or any other trust activity. As trustee, you are responsible for safeguarding the funds for the beneficiaries.

- Pay outstanding bills or debts. If the trustee does not pay bills, he or she may be held personally liable.

- If the trust will generate more than $600 in income from the date of death until all trust assets are distributed (which is generally the case), a tax identification number needs to be obtained for the trust. Where the grantor was their own trustee, their social security number was the tax identification number and the trust income was simply reported on their annual 1040 tax return. But in an irrevocable trust (which is the case where the grantor of a revocable trust dies), the trust is required to report income under its own tax identification number. In a revocable trust, for the year of death, income earned from January 1 through date of death will be reported on the grantor's final Form 1040. Income earned from date of death to date of distribution of all assets will be reported on a Form 1041.

- Be certain that all required tax returns are filed. If the deceased's state of residence has an estate tax, an estate tax return may be necessary. A Federal estate tax return may also be necessary for larger estates. If significant lifetime gifts were made, estate tax returns may also be required.

- File any claims for life insurance, IRA's and other assets needing claims forms. Liquidate any assets that need to be liquidated. Make sure to get professional advice before retitling or liquidating IRA's as there may be serious tax consequences if you make a mistake in this area.

- Create an accounting which begins with the inventory listing all assets existing on the date of death, show all additions of any type, subtract all expenses paid, and show current assets on hand. When you are ready to create the final accounting right before distribution of assets to beneficiaries, it is easiest if assets are placed in a non-interest bearing account. That way values are not constantly changing.

• Have a legal professional prepare a receipt and release form for each beneficiary to sign, simply stating that they have received the inheritance and that they release the trustee from further responsibility or liability.

• Settlement of a trust is easier than going through the probate process since court paperwork and proceedings are avoided. The trustee can access accounts immediately, so debts and expenses may be satisfied without delay and accounts may be consolidated. Most statutory waiting periods are also avoided. Real estate may be listed for sale immediately, as opposed to waiting for months and sometimes years for an executor to be appointed under a will. However, even with a trust, it is very important that specific steps be completed. It is not feasible to list here all steps which would need to be completed in each circumstance. Legal help in designing and terminating trusts streamlines the process, and saves time and money by taking advantage of all tax planning opportunities available to you.

"Joint adventurers, like copartners, owe to one another, while the enterprise continues, the duty of the finest loyalty. Many forms of conduct permissible in a workaday world for those acting at arm's length, are forbidden to those bound by fiduciary ties. A trustee is held to something stricter than the morals of the market place. Not honesty alone, but the punctilio of an honor the most sensitive, is then the standard of behavior. As to this there has developed a tradition that is unbending and inveterate. Uncompromising rigidity has been the attitude of courts of equity when petitioned to undermine the rule of undivided loyalty by the "disintegrating erosion" of particular exceptions...Only thus has the level of conduct for fiduciaries been kept at a level higher than that trodden by the crowd. It will not consciously be lowered by any judgment of this court."

Benjamin N. Cardozo, Meinhard v. Salmon,
249 N.Y. 458, 463-64, 164 N.E. 545 (1928)

59

Using Professional Trustees

Most people who set up living trusts today choose themselves as trustee. However, since trusts continue after the death or disability of the original trustee, a successor trustee must be named. Should you choose an individual trustee, a professional trustee (such as a bank, lawyer or trust company) or a combination of the two?

The advantages of naming an individual are that you know the person and they know you. Presumably, they would act in your best interests knowing how you would wish diverse matters to be handled, including the investment and distribution of your trust assets.

On the other hand, managing a trust may be a complex task. Balancing the income needs of a current beneficiary with the requirement to preserve the capital for future, or contingent, beneficiaries requires knowledge of sound, conservative investment practices. In addition, annual fiduciary returns must be filed for the trust. Individuals often face other commitments or may become disabled or die, leaving the management of the trust in limbo for an extended period of time. Individual trustees may have or develop personality conflicts with siblings. We have seen unresolved childhood conflicts, dormant for years, suddenly reappear with great force in the emotional period following the death of a parent. The issues of money and control often add to these hidden problems. In a similar vein, individual trustees are subject to the influences of their spouses who may be pursuing their own agenda and who are not bound by the "family glue".

Despite parents' best intentions, the chosen trustee may act dishonestly or to their own benefit (self-dealing) and to the detriment of the other trust beneficiaries. Unlike professional trustees, they are not subject to professional or governmental oversight of their actions and they may not have the resources to right a wrong even if they are successfully sued for any wrongful acts.

For continuity, and out of respect for the grantor's choice, the professional trustee will usually retain the attorney or law firm that prepared the trust to settle the estate. The parent's law firm, as opposed to the personal lawyer of one of the children, is more likely to look after the interests of all the beneficiaries in an even-handed manner.

HEALTH AND WELL-BEING FOR OLDER ADULTS

60

Keeping the Lights On

Adapted from author Doug Armey, the following are keys to keeping your brain "lit" as you age.

1. **Flow.** A sedentary life causes brain deterioration. Blood flow to the brain keeps oxygen in your brain cells which gives them life. Keep moving, walking and get some exercise.

2. **Energize.** Junk food clogs your arteries and lowers energy, causing a sedentary lifestyle. Healthy food gives energy to your body and brain. Refuel and brighten the lights.

3. **Recharge.** Lack of enough sleep causes deterioration of the brain. Your brain needs downtime to recharge. Give it enough recharging and keep the lights burning bright.

4. Relax. Constant high stress has damaging effects on the brain and can lead to destructive habits which add further damage. Learn to control stress and let the lights shine.

5. Engage. Like muscles your brain needs exercise. Too often people, after retirement, retire their brains also so they atrophy. Stay engaged, exercise your brain with reading, puzzles and other challenges to keep the lights going on strong.

6. Love. When people grow isolated their brains lack stimulation and they grow dull. Stay connected with family and friends to brighten the lights.

7. Adventure. Many older people lose their zest for new adventures. You don't need to climb Everest just break out of dull routines. Any venture out to new places turns up the lights.

8. Purpose. People can lose interest in life after they have retired, feeling they have no purpose. Look for opportunities to volunteer. Helping others keeps the lights flaming.

61

Accepting What Is

As estate planners, we consistently meet with people who are suffering from traumatic relationships with their children or grandchildren. Children themselves may become estranged or at odds with parents or their siblings. Sometimes, an in-law is involved that seems to turn the client's son or daughter into someone completely different from the child they raised. The pain that these clients are going through is palpable.

Some wise sage once said that all pain comes from resistance. Many of these relationship issues may be difficult or impossible to overcome, but one thing we can all do is work on ourselves -- by accepting what is. Accepting what is does not mean agreeing with or condoning certain behavior. What it does mean is that you stop saying to yourself that it is not fair, it "should" be otherwise, etc.

That will not do you one bit of good and may do you considerable harm. Stress has been called "the silent killer".

We recall reading a pithy quote a while back that went something like this "when someone disappoints you, you have two choices, you can either lower your expectations or walk away". What is disappointment but dashed expectations? Those who learn to expect less are disappointed less.

"Accepting what is" cannot be accomplished overnight. It is a concept or thought process that improves your outlook the more you think about it, work on it and form new neural pathways to forge the new outlook.

Estate planners inevitably becomes "therapists" for their clients because estate planning involves social relationships. Over the years, we have observed that many social problems only occur between the clients two ears. As Shakespeare said in Hamlet "There is nothing good or bad, but thinking makes it so." Forget about what's fair or right and what's not. You are only hurting yourself. The other person is often blissfully unaware of how you're feeling. Michael J. Fox, the actor known for his optimism despite suffering from Parkinson's, put it best when he said "My happiness grows in direct proportion to my acceptance, and in inverse proportion to my expectations".

62

The Caregiver as Invisible Patient

Doctors and other professionals may forget to ask caregivers how they are coping with the care of another. Queries such as whether the caregiver is eating properly, exercising, sleeping enough, becoming depressed or getting any free time may be overlooked. Thankfully, some physicians and other healthcare professionals have noticed the lack of care given to the actual caregivers.

The invisible patient is a person supporting an elderly family member who suffers with dementia, heart disease, diabetes, cancer or a combination of the above. Currently in the United States there are about 50 million people providing this type of care to a loved one over the age of fifty.

Following are some of the risk factors for the invisible patient that should trigger assessment by a doctor: number of hours of caregiving, financial distress, level of cognitive impairment in the patient, level of education of the caregiver, depression, social isolation, a caregiver who lives with the patient, and lack of choice in being a caregiver.

Recommendations for treating physicians include a simple question such as how are you doing, to more complex questions about making other arrangements for care if something were to happen to the caregiver. Doctors are also encouraged to use a toolkit to assess the needs of the caregivers provided by the Family Caregiver Alliance (caregiver.org).

In larger teaching hospitals, social workers and other professionals usually assess caregivers when they bring in loved ones for treatment. Some hospitals require all medical students to spend at least one rotation on the geriatric floor, regardless of career aspirations, to better understand and appreciate the warning signs for caregivers.

Apart from doctors in private practice, others such as community agencies, visiting nurse services, geriatric care managers, and elder law attorneys are all part of the possible safety network to help invisible patients care for their loved ones.

63

Elder Abuse

According to the National Institute on Aging, about one in ten adults over age sixty are abused, neglected or exploited. That is a staggering number. The major forms of abuse are:

• **Physical abuse** happens when someone causes bodily harm by hitting, pushing or slapping. This may also include restraining an older adult against their will, such as locking them in a room.

• **Emotional abuse** includes a caregiver saying hurtful words, yelling, threatening, repeatedly ignoring the older adult or keeping that person from seeing close friends and relatives.

• **Neglect** occurs when the caregiver does not respond to the older adult's needs. This may include physical, emotional and social needs or withholding food, medications or access to health care.

- **Abandonment** is leaving an older adult who needs help alone without planning for their care.

- **Financial abuse** occurs when money or belongings are stolen from an older adult. It can include forging checks, taking someone else's retirement or Social Security benefits, using a person's credit cards and bank accounts without their permission, changing names on a will or trust, bank account, life insurance policy or title to a house without permission.

- **Financial neglect** occurs when an older adult's financial responsibilities such as paying rent or a mortgage, medical expenses or insurance, utility bills or property taxes are ignored, and the person's bills are not paid.

- **Financial exploitation** is the misuse, mismanagement or exploitation of property, belongings or assets. This includes using an older adult's assets without consent, under false pretenses or through intimidation and/or manipulation.

If you see signs of abuse, try talking with the older adult to find out what's going on. Many seniors are either too ashamed or fearful of retribution from the abuser if they report the mistreatment. If you see something, say something -- report what you see to your county's adult protective services office and they will investigate.

64

Positive Aspects of Aging

Aging provides its own rewards, which only those who experience it really know, as the following quotes show.

"Getting old is like climbing a mountain; you get a little out of breath, but the view is much better!"
-- Ingrid Bergman

"Nothing is inherently and invincibly young except spirit. And spirit can enter a human being perhaps better in the quiet of old age and dwell there more undisturbed than in turmoil of adventure."
-- George Santayana

"The older I get, the greater power I seem to have to help the world; I am like a snowball - the further I am rolled the more I gain."
-- Susan B. Anthony

"Why not just embrace it, go along with it and welcome it?"
-- Helen Mirren

"I believe the second half of one's life is meant to be better than the first half. The first half is finding out how you do it. And the second half is enjoying it." -- Frances Lear

"Beautiful young people are accidents of nature, but beautiful old people are works of art."-- Eleanor Roosevelt

"The complete life, the perfect pattern, includes old age as well as youth and maturity. The beauty of the morning and the radiance of noon are good, but it would be a very silly person who drew the curtains and turned on the light in order to shut out the tranquility of the evening. Old age has its pleasures, which, though different, are not less than the pleasures of youth." - W. Somerset Maugham

"There is a fountain of youth; it is your mind, your talents, the creativity you bring to your life and the lives of people you love. When you learn to tap this source, you will truly have defeated age." -- Sophia Loren

65

Book Review: "Healthy at 100" by John Robbins

Subtitled "How You Can - At Any Age - Dramatically Increase Your Life Span and Your Health Span", Mr. Robbins' book is one that appealed to us for a very specific reason. So many of our clients over the years have said, "Oh no! I wouldn't want to live to 100", the assumption being that they would inevitably be infirm.

Our culture, in television and movies, reinforces this thinking by portraying the elderly as feeble, unproductive, and out of sorts. Elders are demeaned with stereotypes as being unworthy of consideration or positive regard, according to Robbins.

Baby boomers today range in ages from 63 - 78. It's time to shed these old myths. Author Robbins describes four cultures in the world as follows:

Abkhasia: Ancients of the Caucasus where people are healthier at ninety then most of us are at middle age.

Vilcabamba: The Valley of Eternal Youth where heart disease and dementia do not exist.

Hunta: A people who dance in their nineties where cancer, diabetes and asthma are unknown.

The Centenarians of Okinawa: Where more people live to 100 than anywhere in the world.

The major takeaway from these ancient cultures are the diets, physical activities, social ties and respect for the elderly these societies engender to account for their extended life expectancies.

Perhaps one of Robbins best lines is "the whiter the bread, the sooner you're dead". When whole wheat flour is refined into white flour here is just some of what is lost: protein 25%, fiber 95%, calcium 56%, iron 84%, vitamins, an average of over 70%. The long-term perils of eating too much sugar are discussed: obesity, kidney stones, osteoporosis, heart disease and diabetes.

It's never too late to change. As the book says "people don't grow old. When they stop growing, they become old"

Taking a deeper dive, the book cites a preeminent expert on aging, John W. Rowe, M.D., Chairman of the MacArthur Foundation Research Network on Successful Aging who explains: "The bottom line is very clear: with rare exceptions, only about 30 percent of physical aging can be blamed on genes...MacArthur Research provides very strong evidence that we are, in large part, responsible for our own old age."

Take the example of longest lived people in the world -- the Okinawans "When Okinawans move elsewhere and adopt the diets of their new locations, they get the same diseases at the same rates and die at the same ages, as the people whose customs they embrace. The life expectancy of Okinawans who move to Brazil, for example, drops seventeen years."

"Diseases of affluence" -- including diabetes, coronary heart diseases and many forms of cancer are all linked to animal-based diets. Foods that decrease cholesterol levels are soy products, whole grains, fruits, vegetables, peas and beans. "As a result of the vast amount of information gathered...the scientific evidence indicates that a diet based on plant foods with a minimal amount of food derived from animals as the ideal diet for human beings." Since almost all the cells in your body continually regenerate, "steps you can take" provides a guide "so what you eat today literally becomes your body tomorrow."

Next up are physical activities. The Vilcabamba have a saying, that "each of us has two doctors -- the left leg and the right leg." People become passive and then the less they move the harder it becomes to do so. However, "those who think they have no time for bodily exercise will sooner or later have to find time for illness."

Apart from the effect that diet and exercise have in extending healthful life are the mental and social aspects. As noted author Norman Cousins wrote, "Death is not the greatest loss in life. The greatest loss in life is what dies inside us while we live."

Robbins advises that the old saying "use it or lose it" applies as much to the brain as it does to muscles. Keys to cognitive health are engagement with life and having goals and things to look forward to.

"The elders most likely to experience dementia are those who spend their days watching television or wandering aimlessly around the mall. On the other hand, those who are contributing to the lives of others, who are engaged in some way in making the world a better or more beautiful place, not only more fully retain their cognitive faculties as they grow older, but often find themselves expanding into new levels of awareness and understanding."

Finally, the old Tina Turner song "What's Love Got to Do With It?" comes to mind. The answer? A lot. Studies show that self-absorbed people are far less healthy. One doctor advises "Listen with regard when others talk. Give your time and energy to others, let others have their way, do things for reasons other than furthering your own needs."

One study of a group of women suffering from metastatic breast cancer showed that those who participated in a support group lived an average of 37 months while those who went it alone lived an average of 17 months. The women in the support group also experienced fewer mood swings and less pain and fear.

"Modern research is now repeatedly finding that your relationship with others is medically potent. Your connections with the significant people in your life -- if they are positive and loving -- can prevent stress-induced illness, greatly contribute to your health and healing, and add many years to your life.

66

Polypharmacy in Older Adults

According to the National Institute on Aging (NIA) polypharmacy is the use of multiple drugs to treat diseases and other health conditions. Polypharmacy is common in older adults, many of whom have two or more chronic conditions, and about a third of whom take five or more prescription drugs. Often, these different powerful drugs have been prescribed by different doctors. Some drugs mask or neutralize others, some are dangerously incompatible with others and some may worsen conditions that naturally occur in the aging population -- such as loss of appetite, less efficient digestive systems and increased cardiovascular risk.

Inappropriate polypharmacy -- the use of excessive or unnecessary medications -- increases the risk of adverse drug effects, including falls and cognitive impairment. Harmful drug interactions and drug-disease interactions may also occur, where a medication prescribed to treat one condition worsens or creates a new one.

Enter the new field of "deprescribing". The NIA is developing a network of scientists to advance the field of deprescribing to improve the quality of care and health outcomes for older adults. According to Parag Goyal, MD, "despite its role as an integral part of patient-centric and goal-concordant prescribing practice, deprescribing is not frequently incorporated into routine clinical practice".

In seeking to view medications in a way that is more patient-centered and less disease-oriented and guideline-driven, the NIA advises talking to your doctors about deprescribing if you feel a drug is not working or is causing harmful side effects. Make sure to bring a list of all medications you are currently taking, prescription and over-the-counter. Ask if there are any that may not be necessary.

For the American Geriatrics Society's (AGS) list of medications that older people should avoid or use with caution, google "Beers List". The Beers List is recommended for assessing your medications, however AGS advises not to stop taking any medication without talking to your doctor first.

67

Better Sleep for Older Adults

While sleep is essential for mental and physical health, aging presents some sleep challenges. About half of all seniors report a sleep problem such as taking longer to fall asleep, shorter sleep, waking up often and napping more and longer. As we age, our body clock deteriorates and melatonin (a sleep inducing chemical) levels decline. To increase the amount and quality of sleep, the three main factors are (1) routine, (2) sleeping environment, and (3) diet and exercise.

Routine: A consistent evening routine works best for sleeping. Going to bed at the same time and "winding down" makes a considerable difference. Avoid uses of electronic devices such as smartphones and television as they emit "blue light" which inhibits melatonin production and can upset body rhythms. Blue light blocking lenses may avoid this problem.

Sleeping Environment: Cooling down the bedroom can lead to better sleep. If the thermostat is out of your control, a fan will help. Light should be just enough to allow you not to trip and fall should you need to get out of bed. Darkness options are blackout blinds or curtains and covering any electronics that emit light. An eye mask can work wonders too. Outside noises or partners who snore can disturb sleep. Consider "white noise" machines or spa-like recordings to help you sleep. Like the eye mask for light, consider ear plugs for noise. While a firm, comfortable mattress and quality pillows with breathable fabrics are essential, there are other high-tech options that may assist, such as mattress and pillows that adjust their temperature as yours changes. Many people report a weighted blanket works wonders.

Diet and Exercise: Caffeine and sugar are stimulants that prevent sleep. While alcohol can help you fall asleep, the sleep quality suffers. Eating earlier and drinking less will both help your body get to sleep and stay asleep. Moving around more, either by doing chores, taking a few trips up and down the stairs or simply sitting down and getting up a few times avoids the sedentary lifestyle that causes insomnia. Few things promote sleep better than a walk outside in the fresh air. To learn more visit purple.com/blog/senior-sleep-guide.

68

Death with Dignity: Hospice Care

The announcement by 98 year old Jimmy Carter, our longest-lived president, that he was opting for hospice care at home instead of additional medical intervention, is in keeping with the trend towards dying with dignity. Hospice care arises when an illness is either no longer responding to medical treatment, no medical treatment is available, or the patient has decided they want to transition from treatments intended to prolong quantity of life to treatments intended to improve quality of life.

One of the great misconceptions about hospice care is that it is the cessation of medical care. Dr. Sunita Puri, author of "That Good Night: Life and Medicine in the Eleventh Hour" defines hospice care as "intensive comfort-focused care, provided with the goal of minimizing the physical, emotional and spiritual suffering that patients and their families experience when somebody has possibly six months or less to live." While hospice can usually take place at home it can also be in a facility and is paid for by Medicare Hospice Benefit.

The hospice "team" consists of (1) a nurse to assess and manage pain and provide hands-on-care, (2) a social worker, to offer emotional support and help with planning, (3) a physician to interface with the patient's primary physician and consult on pain and symptom management and make house calls, (4) a hospice aide to help with personal care needs, such as bathing, (5) clergy to offer spiritual support, (6) volunteers to help in a variety of ways, and (7) a bereavement specialist to provide grief and loss counseling.

Regrettably, hospice care in the US averages only about three weeks, due to the fact that people are reluctant to talk about topics like suffering, quality of life and whether treatments are adding to or detracting from someone's quality of life. Delaying those conversations leads to very late referrals to hospice.

As Dr. Puri points out, "Hospice is not about giving up...hospice is about acknowledging where your body is at, at a given stage of illness, and honoring that and honoring the person that you are, which is distinct from the illness you are suffering...hospice attempts to maximize dignity and minimize suffering."

69

Aging Life Care Managers (ALCM)

An Aging Life Care Manager (ALCM) is a health and human services specialist who acts as a guide and advocate for families who are caring for older relatives or disabled adults. The expertise of ALCM's can be summarized into these knowledge areas.

Health and Disability. From physical problems to mental health and dementia-related problems, ALCM's interact with the health care system by attending doctor appointments and facilitating communication between doctor, client and family. They help determine types of services – such as home health and hospice – that are right for a client and assist in engaging and monitoring those services.

Financial. Reviewing or overseeing bill paying or consulting with a client's accountant or agent under a power of attorney. ALCM's provide information on Federal and state entitlements, connecting families to local programs when appropriate. They also help clients and families with insurance concerns, claims and applications.

Housing. ALCM's help families and clients evaluate and select appropriate level of housing or residential options.

Families. ALCM's help families adjust, cope and problem-solve around long-distance and in-home caregiving, addressing care concerns, internal conflicts and differences of opinion about long-term care planning.

Local Resources. ALCM's know the specifics of the local resources in their communities and know how those services are accessed.
In addition, ALCM's act as advocates for the client's interests and are a valuable resource when emergencies arise. A care plan, tailored for each individual's situation, is prepared which may be modified as circumstances change. ALCM's are certified by the Aging Life Care Association which maintains a list of ALCM's by zip code at aginglifecare.org.

70

Book Review: "Happiness is a Choice You Make" by John Leland

In his book, subtitled "Lessons From a Year Among the Oldest Old", journalist John Leland takes us on a journey into uncharted territory. Mr. Leland spent a year with six elderly New Yorkers, exploring their lives.

He divides the book into the first six chapters chronicling the years spent with each of the six -- John, 97, living in the same Manhattan apartment for forty-six years, the last six of them alone after the death of his partner; Fred, 87, a World War II vet and retired civil servant living in a three-story walk up; Helen, 90, living in The Hebrew Home in the Bronx, dating Howie, living down the hall; Ping, 89, providing an Asian perspective, living in a rent-controlled apartment with a Medicaid paid home attendant for seven hours a day; Ruth, a feisty 90, in assisted living in Sheepshead Bay, Brooklyn and, finally, Jonas, 92, an active filmmaker and writer.

Along with the author, we live the lives of these six people from getting up in the morning to going to bed at night. "How did they get through the day, and what were their hopes for the morrow? How did they manage their medications, their children, and their changing bodies..." Further, says Mr. Leland "All had lost something: mobility, vision, spouses, children, peers, memory but few had lost everything." What the author found was that the "oldest old" are not a different species, as so many people see them, but rather much the same as you and me -- getting up each morning with wants and needs and doing the best they can with what they have. Nevertheless, older people report a greater sense of well-being and fewer negative emotions than younger people. "Experience helps older people moderate their expectations and makes them more resilient when things don't go as hoped." We learn the many ways his six seniors chose to be happy.

The final six chapters detail the lessons learned from each of the elders. These are worlds well worth exploring. As Ruth said to her daughter one day "I was your age, you were never my age."

71

Battling the Epidemic of Loneliness

According to former Surgeon General Vivek H. Murthy, MD, loneliness poses real threats to both mental and physical health, including depression and anxiety, addictions, heart disease and dementia. His book "Together" reveals that loneliness affects about one-quarter of adult Americans, and "The reality is that loneliness is a natural signal that our body gives us, similar to hunger, thirst. And that's how important human connection is." Such is the public health crisis, that in the UK the government has appointed a Minister of Loneliness to help combat the problem.

One of the best ways to overcome loneliness is to volunteer. AARP Foundation Experience Corps reports that 85% of volunteers felt their lives had improved through their volunteering efforts.

Here are some suggestions and resources gleaned from Val Walker's ground-breaking book "400 Friends and No One to Call" subtitled "Breaking Through Isolation and Building Community."

- Be patient and compassionate. It takes time and understanding to build solid relationships.
- Cast a wide net for meeting new people. It takes a lot of "nos" to get to a "yes".
- Stay open-minded and not too fixated on who fits your "tribe". You might be surprised who welcomes you into their world.
- If volunteering, look for opportunities to combine volunteering with socializing and avoid volunteering that is isolating (like stuffing envelopes).
- Have a "calling card" with your contact information.
- Go to newcomers groups or network meet ups (meetup.com) to meet people who are eager to build new relationships.
- Consider "house sharing". One of the many websites for older women is silvernest.com.
- AARP's website for fighting isolation, connect2affect.org, has many evidence-based suggestions to help people get more involved in their communities.
- For women living in New York City or Long Island, visit ttnwomen.org.

Dr. Stephanie Cacioppo, a leading researcher on loneliness, advocates the GRACE method: gratitude, reciprocity, altruism, choice and enjoyment. In other words, be grateful for what you have, give and take help from others, and enjoy your life. Choice refers to the fact that we are responsible for our choices -- you either choose to do something about your loneliness -- or not.

72

Health Benefits of Forgiveness

Each one of us experience countless injustices in the course of everyday living. Like other experiences, it is not the experience itself so much that counts, but how you process it. The Mayo Clinic addresses the health benefits of "forgiveness" which they define as "an intentional decision to let go of resentment and anger". Letting go of grudges and bitterness can lead to:

- Healthier relationships
- Improved mental health
- Less anxiety, stress and hostility
- Fewer symptoms of depression
- Lower blood pressure
- A stronger immune system
- Improved heart health

- Improved self-esteem
- Better sleep

Everett Worthington, Profession Emeritus of Psychology, Virginia Commonwealth University, provides a free workbook at evworthington-forgiveness.com to aid those for whom forgiveness may be difficult (most of us!), focusing on the REACH method.

Recall: Recall the hurt. Look at the incident in an objective way and don't try to push aside your feelings. '

Empathize: Empathize with the offender without excusing the action or invalidating your own feels. Maybe the person was having a bad day or was raised in dire circumstances.

Altruistic gift: Give the altruistic gift of forgiveness. Think about a time when you were rude or harsh, and recognize that everyone has shortcomings.

Commit: Make a decision to forgive. You can write a letter that you don't send to help yourself make the commitment.

Hold: Hold on to forgiveness. Memories of the transgression or event won't change. But how you react to those feelings will.

"Holding on to anger is like grasping a hot coal with the intent of throwing it at someone else; you are the one who gets burned". -- Buddha

73

Book Review: "Let's Talk About Death" by Michael Hebb

In his invitation and guide to life's most important conversation, as he puts it, author Michael Hebb seeks to address the fact that "the way we die in the modern age is broken." Almost unique to American culture, the denial of death has ripple effects in depleting our skills to discuss death and to process the loss of a loved one.

Perhaps this is why (1) although 80% of Americans say they want to die at home, only 20% do, and (2) the leading cause of bankruptcy in the United States is the cost of end-of-life care. Most people do not want extreme measures that only prolong suffering leading to death. However, so few of us have talked to our families about our wishes nor have we been asked, leading to the medicalization of end-of-life.

Given the right framework, these conversations can be liberating and even transforming -- bringing people together and reminding us what really matters. While death is often tragic and terrible, there are opportunities to learn and grow -- by making us more aware of life's precious gift, making us kinder and bringing us closer to one another.

While talking about death may require planting the seed and waiting for the right time, being patient while someone slowly opens up, these conversations make people's lives better as well as the lives of their loved ones.

Although we carefully plan all of life's major transitions, graduations, weddings, etc., "to deny our end-of-life the same level of consideration denies a tremendous part of us, perhaps the most important part: that we are in fact mortal," the author writes.

With death everything changes in the lives of those left behind. Death also brings birth -- birth of memories, new understandings and new relationships. The author helps us get better acquainted with our "constant companion" in a way that helps move our lives forward.

74

Strength Training for Seniors

A few years ago, your author found that he was having trouble doing the yard work and carrying the trash to the curb. I was getting weaker with age and realized that this trend was only going to go in one direction. So I decided to reverse the decline with strength training. Putting in just three hours a week, I am now stronger than I was thirty years ago.

The British Journal of Sports Medicine reports that just thirty to sixty minutes a week of strength or "resistance" training leads to a ten to twenty percent decrease in heart disease, cancer and mortality. It also increases cognitive function and decreases anxiety and depression. Better yet, you can carry in the groceries or climb the stairs without getting exhausted!

Strength training doesn't mean you have to go to the gym and start lifting heavy weights. Just doing push-ups, planks, squats, walking up stairs, etc. are all forms of resistance training. You don't even have to change your clothing, so long as you have enough room to move.

Instead of sitting for hours on end watching television, how about simply pulling your shoulders back, straightening your back and then getting up and sitting down for ten or fifteen minutes. Add in some push-ups and planks and you have both upper and lower body work-outs.

Start slow and build up your strength and repetitions. It is amazing how quickly the body responds at any age, even in one's nineties. As my mother used to say when I was growing up "Go outside and do a muscle a favor!".

Proper form is essential to avoiding injury and getting the most out of your efforts. A regular personal trainer works wonders. But if that is outside your budget, then consider just a couple of sessions to develop a custom plan that you can continue on your own.

Switching from a sedentary lifestyle to a workout schedule including aerobics, like brisk walking, is "comparable to smoking v. not smoking" according to the British Journal.

75

Book Review: "Successful Aging" by Daniel J. Levitin

In his best-selling book, "Successful Aging", Daniel J. Levitin, Professor Emeritus of Psychology and Neuroscience at McGill University (your author's alma mater), shows how the brain is formed and how it changes, in surprisingly positive ways, as we age.

The author notes that Freud said that the two most important things in life are healthy relationships and meaningful work.

Socialization is crucial to maintaining our mental acuity. "Navigating the complex mores and potential pitfalls of dealing with another human being, someone who has their own needs, opinions, and sensitivities, is about the most complex thing we humans can do. It exercises vast neural networks, keeping them tuned up, in shape, and ready to fire. In a good conversation, we listen, we empathize. And empathy is healthful, activating networks throughout the brain."

If working is not a viable option then volunteering reduces mental decline. "Volunteering at a local organization, community center, or hospital can have all the benefits of continuing to work: a sense of self-worth and accomplishment, and the daily interaction with others that causes the brain to light up. The data reveal that volunteering is associated with reduced symptoms of depression, better self-reported health, fewer functional limitations, and lower mortality."

The author concludes "Gratitude is an important and often overlooked emotion and state of mind. Gratitude causes us to focus on what's good about our lives rather than what's bad shifting our outlook to the positive...psychology's focus on disorders and problems of adjustment was ignoring much of what makes life worth living. Positive psychology has found that people who practice gratitude feel happier."

Please note that a science background is helpful in understanding the four hundred pages that make up "Successful Aging".

76

Book Review: "Die With Zero" by Bill Perkins

In "Die with Zero", subtitled "Getting All That You Can from Your Money and Your Life", retired engineer Bill Perkins takes an analytical view about making your life grow as opposed to making your money grow. Letting opportunities pass you by for fear of squandering money leads many to squander their lives instead.

Instead of just keeping on earning and earning to maximize wealth, too many of us don't give nearly as much thought as to maximizing what they can get out of that wealth -- including what they can give to others while they are living, instead of waiting until they die.

As opposed to spending money on things, which excitement depreciates over time, the author advocates spending on experiences, which grow in value over time, due to the "memory dividend". Perkins advocates a systematic approach for eliminating the fear of running out of money (the main reason people oversave and underenjoy) while maximizing your and your loved ones enjoyment of that money.

Being that the main idea is that your life is the sum of your experiences, you should put some thought into planning the kind of experiences you want. If you die with significant wealth but a scarcity of experiences, you worked a lot of hours just to accumulate money that you either never used or were too old to use.

You can waste your life by underspending. Life is not only about "accumulating", it is also about "decumulating" or using the money to maximize your life which, in the end, is nothing more than the memories you make.

In a similar vein, giving inheritances early maximizes the impact of those inheritances on the recipients' quality of life. The average age of heirs being about sixty, the money usually arrives too late to do the most good.

Your time is limited. The chief regrets of the dying are that they didn't live their dreams more and spent too much time working, missing out on relationships and life experiences.

77

Book Review: "The Good Life" by Robert Waldinger, MD and Marc Schulz, PhD

"The Good Life" reports on the Harvard Study of Adult Development, the longest scientific study of happiness ever done. Tracking the lives of hundreds of participants for over 80 years, the report concludes that it is the strength of our relationships with friends, relatives and co-workers that most determine quality of life, health and longevity.

Regarding older adults, the authors note that time is suddenly very precious. Questions arise such as:

- How much time do I have left?
- How long will I stay healthy?
- Am I losing it mentally?
- Who do I want to spend this limited time with?

- Have I had a good enough life?
- What do I regret?

"The fewer moments we have to look forward to in life, the more valuable they become. Past grievances and preoccupations often dissipate...research has shown that human beings are never so happy as in the late years of their lives. We get better at maximizing highs and minimizing lows. We feel less hassled by the little things that go wrong, and we get better at knowing when something is important and when it's not. The value of positive experiences far outweighs the cost of negative experiences, and we prioritize things that bring us joy. In short, we're emotionally wiser, and that wisdom helps us thrive."

We learn that neglected relationships, like muscles, atrophy. Our social life, being a living system, needs exercise. Further, the reason social relationships are so valuable has a biological basis -- a means of protection from predators. Without meaningful relationships, we remain in a state of stress, often unknown to us.

Make the effort. Most of us have friends and relatives who energize us and who we don't see enough. As Mark Twain said, "There isn't time, so brief is life, for bickerings, apologies, heartburnings, callings to account. There is only time for loving, and but an instant, so to speak, for that".

78

Increasing Your Emotional Intelligence

The philosopher Epictetus said "Men are disturbed not by events, but by the views they take of them." Arising out of "The Good Life", previously reviewed here, comes the W.I.S.E.R. model for reacting to emotionally challenging situations.

Watch. Initial impressions are powerful but may be incomplete. There is usually more to see. When the impression and the emotional response start to interact, take a moment to pause and thoughtfully observe the situation to prevent a potentially harmful reflexive response. As they say in psychiatry "Don't just do something, sit there."

Interpret. We are all seeing the world through our own eyes -- what is happening, why it is happening and how it affects us. Our reality is not necessarily that of others. Thinking that a situation is all about us often leads to misunderstanding. When your emotions start to bubble up, it indicates you have something important at stake -- a goal, an insecurity or a vital relationship. Figuring out what's at stake will allow you to interpret the situation better.

Select. Having watched, interpreted and re-interpreted, you must select your response. Instead of reacting reflexively out of stress, slowing down allows us to choose from more options. As "The Good Life" says "Given what's at stake and the resources at my disposal, what can I do in this situation? What would be a good outcome here? And what is the likelihood that things will go well if I respond this way instead of that way?"

Engage. Now you are ready to respond more purposefully -- aligning with who you are and what you want to accomplish. You've observed and interpreted the situation, taken some time to consider the possibilities and their likelihood of success, and you then execute your strategy.

Reflect. "How did that work out? Did I make things better or worse? Have I learned something new about the challenge I'm facing and about the best response? Reflecting on our response to a challenge can yield dividends for the future. It's in learning from experience that we fully grow wiser."

79

Multivitamins and Older Adults

About one-third of Americans 60 and older take multivitamins. Perhaps the remaining two-thirds should as well. According to a major new study, the second of its kind to reach the same conclusion, taking multivitamins over age sixty delays the onset of memory loss by about 3 years.

The study used a commonly available multivitamin, Centrum Silver, which contains vitamins D, A, B12, thiamine, riboflavin, manganese and other substances, although it was noted that any high-quality multivitamin would do just as well.

A Washington Post article about these findings quotes JoAnn Manson of Harvard Medical School "Older adults are very concerned about preserving cognition and memory, so this is a very important finding. They are looking for safe and effective prevention strategies. The fact that two separate studies came to similar conclusions is remarkable."

Another expert cited was Andrew Budson, Professor of Neurology at Boston University "This study is groundbreaking. Low levels of vitamins B1 -- also known as thiamine -- B12 and D are associated with cognitive decline. That a simple multivitamin can slow cognitive decline while they are aging normally is quite exciting, as it is something almost everyone can do."

The reasons that multivitamin "therapy" is so effective is explained by Paul E. Schultz, Professor Neurology at McGovern Medical School, Houston -- the brain requires a lot of vitamins and minerals to function properly. While the goal is to maintain nutrition through a healthy and balanced diet, as we age our bodies may be unable to absorb sufficient levels of the essential elements. In addition, some medications interfere with the absorption of nutrients. Schulz states "Think of a complicated engine that requires lots of specialty parts and needs them all. We regularly see people who are deficient in nutrients come in with cognitive impairment."

If you are on medications, it is recommended that you consult your doctor before you try a supplement, as some vitamins may interfere with those medications.

80

Book Review: "Outlive: The Science & Art of Longevity" by Peter Attia, MD

In his bestselling book, Dr. Attia challenges conventional medical thinking. Instead of treating illnesses, he focuses far greater attention on preventing them from occurring. Quoting Desmond Tutu, he says "There comes a point where we need to stop just pulling people out of the river. We need to go upstream and find out why they're falling in". Being that there is far less profit in preventative medicine -- both for the medical profession and the pharmaceutical industry -- he is up against considerable resistance.

Longevity means not only how long you live but how well you live -- quantity and quality of life -- which he terms "lifespan and healthspan".

"Outlive" is an operating manual for increasing both aspects of longevity which, the author points out, is far more malleable than we realize. The beauty of acquiring this knowledge is that you can start at any age and greatly improve your prospects. You just need to know how.

To avoid the gravitational pull of aging, we have to take steps to improve our physical and cognitive function. The prescription for working and acting like someone one or even two decades younger than your chronological age or, in other words, outliving your life expectancy and exceeding society's expectations of what later life looks like, fills these pages.

As the author states, "This is our objective: to delay death, and to get the most out of our extra years. The rest of our lives becomes a time to relish rather than to dread."

Dr. Attia suggests that as we age, you either surrender to decline or come up with a plan, starting now, not only to get more out of life but to stave off The Four Horsemen of The Apocalypse: cancer, heart disease, diabetes and Alzheimer's.

While medicine currently relies on procedures, like surgery, and medications, this new approach advocates five domains: exercise, nutrition, sleep, emotional health and, grouped together, drugs, hormones and supplements.

In his book, Dr. Attia describes the tactics necessary for the "compression of morbidity" -- meaning shrinking the period of decline at the end of life and increasing the length of healthy life. To live longer without disease rather than simply extending the duration of disease.

Centuries of observations have shown that simply eating less extends life and prevents the onset of disease. As the old saying goes, "Eat breakfast like a king, lunch like a prince, and supper like a pauper."

Tips for avoiding cardiovascular disease, including a review of the current cholesterol lowering medications, is provided.

Cancer is analyzed for how it works in the body and the current as well as promising future therapies, while advocating for the best cancer treatment of all --"early detection".

Whereas Alzheimer's and other neurodegenerative diseases were, until recently, thought to be unpreventable, that is no longer true. While quality of sleep and nutrition play a role in preventing cognitive decline, nothing compares to exercise -- both strength training and aerobic exercise -- which reduce inflammation and oxidative stress and increase vascular function.

Seventy-seven percent of the US population does not exercise at all. Going from zero to just ninety minutes a week reduces your risk of dying from all causes by 14 percent -- something that no drug can do. Regular exercisers live as much as a decade longer than sedentary people.

Among the many other longevity issues that Dr. Attia addresses are the powerful effects of sleep on health. Poor sleep wreaks havoc on our metabolism. Sleeping less than six hours a night raises the risk of a heart attack by 20% and is a powerful potential cause of cognitive decline.

Emotional health is given its due because the most important ingredient in the whole longevity equation is the "why". Why do we want to live longer? For whom?

Instead of looking at the quest for longevity as a grim, desperate task the author found that by attending to his emotional health he was enhancing his life and looking forward to the future. Quoting one of the survivors of the Miracle on the Hudson, where Captain Sullenberger safely ditched his jetliner into the Hudson River without any loss of life, he says "If you want someone's true age, listen to them. If they talk about the past and then talk about all the things that happened that they did, they've gotten old. If they talk about their dreams, their aspirations, what they're still looking forward to -- they're young". It only make sense that nature would tend to keep around those who are needed and useful.

This is a lengthy and highly technical book that explores all of the concepts discussed in great detail, along with prescriptions for improvement in all of these areas. It is not an easy read but a very worthwhile addition to the ever burgeoning literature on life extension. As Muhammad Ali said "I never won a fight in the ring; I always won in preparation".

81

The Attitude of Gratitude

"Joy is the simplest form of gratitude." -- Karl Barth

Gratitude has to do with appreciation. Appreciation means to add value to. Things that appreciate tend to grow, just as being grateful for something or someone raises its or their value in our estimation. Even though, at any given time, countless more things are going right than going wrong in most of our lives, too many of us focus more on what's going wrong and take for granted what's going right -- our health, our loved ones, our resources.

Psychologist Robert A. Emmons led the first major scientific study of gratitude over twenty years ago. He found that "Gratitude heals, energizes and changes lives. It is the prism through which we view life in terms of gifts, givers, goodness and grace".

About five years ago, the John Templeton Foundation sponsored a major study by The Greater Good Science Center at The University of California (UC) entitled "The Science of Gratitude" examining the biological roots of gratitude, the various benefits that accompany gratitude, and the ways people can cultivate feelings of gratitude in their daily lives. Overall, the study concluded that grateful people are healthier mentally and physically.

"As early at 63 BC, Cicero remarked "Gratitude is not only the greatest of all virtues, but the parent of all the others." The UC study bears this out, finding that gratitude is associated with patience, humility and wisdom. Grateful people are also more generous and have better personal and professional relationships.

A key finding is Sara Algoe's "find-remind-and-bind" theory of the importance in building and supporting close relationships "By helping people recognize the thoughtfulness of others, gratitude helps them 'find' or identify people who are good candidates for quality future relationships; it also helps 'remind' people of the goodness of their existing relationships; and it 'binds' them to their partners and friends by making them feel appreciated and encouraging them to engage in behaviors that will help prolong their relationships." "Gratitude interventions" is the term used for cultivating the attitude of gratitude in our lives.

An app called "Gratitude Plus" allows you to (1) share gratitude with your favorite people (2) easily reflect on the good in your life (3) create groups with friends and family (4) hear from people around the world (5) track progress and understand trends (6) use streaks to build a habit (7) get creative with a variety of prompts, and (8) stay positive with daily affirmations. As to the latter, your writer has found reading daily affirmations to be an invaluable resource. Daily affirmations help one maintain a positive mindset. The great motivational speaker Zig Ziglar notably said that "People say that motivation doesn't last. Neither does bathing – that's why we recommend it daily". Daily positive affirmations may be found by googling "daily affirmations" and choosing one of the services that appeals to you.

The UC analysis of 38 gratitude studies concluded that "gratitude interventions can have positive benefits for people in terms of their well-being, happiness, life satisfaction, grateful mood, grateful disposition, and positive affect, and they can result in decreases in depressive symptoms".

"Nine-tenths of wisdom is appreciation. Go find someone's hand and squeeze it while there's time." – Dale Dauten

82

Book Review: "Flourish" by Martin E. P. Seligman

In 1998, as President of the American Psychological Association, Martin Seligman recognized that psychology was only addressing psychological "problems" such as depression, anxiety, schizophrenia, personality disorders, etc. Seligman became known as the father of positive psychology by proposing that psychology supplement its venerable goal with a new goal: exploring what makes life worth living and building and enabling conditions of a life worth living.

Positive psychology's content – happiness, flow, meaning, love, gratitude, accomplishment, growth, better relationships – constitutes human flourishing.

Well-being is more than happiness, itself a somewhat vague term. The measures of well-being are (1) positive emotion (2) engagement (3) meaning (4) positive relationships, and (5) accomplishment.

Seligman likens well-being to a "construct" like the weather. It has several measurable elements, each contributing to the "construct", be it well-being or the weather, but none alone being well-being or the weather itself. For the weather these are: temperature, humidity, wind speed, barometric pressure, and so on. For well-being, those who are the most positive, have the most engagement, and the most meaning in life are the happiest and have the most life satisfaction.

Breaking down the elements, positive emotion relates closest to what we think of as happiness – a pleasant and satisfying life. Engagement corresponds to "being in the flow" or so absorbed in what you are doing that you lose sense of time and place. "Meaning" refers to serving something larger than oneself. Your writer has previously posited that if you're feeling unhappy try doing something for someone else and, sure enough, Seligman writes "we scientists have found that doing a kindness produces the single most reliable momentary increase in well-being of any exercise we have tested."

For evolutionary reasons, most people are wired to dwell on negative events rather than positive ones. It helped our ancient ancestors survive the far greater and more varied dangers than we face today. As Seligman notes, "So to overcome our brains' natural catastrophic bent, we need to work on and practice this skill of thinking about what went well...every night for the next week, set aside ten minutes before you go to sleep. Write down three things that went well." These may be of varying levels of importance but the "why" is an important element in stimulating gratitude. As the author says, "The odds are that you will be less depressed, happier, and addicted to this exercise six months from now."

Professor Seligman describes this and other gratitude exercises that his students report as "life-changing."

Another example of an exercise that cultivates optimism and hope is to see bad events as temporary, changeable and local. Here, the client thinks of three doors that closed on her. What doors opened?

Working with psychotherapy and drugs for over forty years, Seligman had never experienced the improvements in mental health that he observed with his positive psychology experiments – all of which led him to the realization of the dirty little secret of drugs and psychotherapy – they are not about cure, they are about short-term treatments. Not only that, but every drug has the property that "once you stop taking it, you are back to square one, and recurrence and relapse are the rule."

Relieving the patient of suffering misery and negative symptoms -- the disabling conditions of life – is not remotely the same as building the enabling conditions of life – to flourish we must have positive emotion, meaning, accomplishment and positive relationships. Seligman found that once he helped a patient get rid of all his anxiety, anger and sadness he never got a happy patient. Instead, he got an empty patient and that is because the skills of flourishing are something over and above the skills of minimizing suffering. Seligman writes "Positive psychology is the study of positive emotion, of engagement, of meaning, of positive accomplishment, and of good relationships. It attempts to measure, clarify and build these five aspects of life...positive psychology is rooted in scientific experience that it works."

After showing the amazing effects of positive emotion on children's development, the flourishing of businesses and on morale and performance in the military, Seligman concludes that "the entire thrust of this book is that optimal performance is tied to good well-being; the higher the positive morale, the better the performance."

Post-traumatic growth is analyzed beginning with "the ancient wisdom that personal transformation is characterized by renewed appreciation of being alive, enhanced personal strength, acting on new possibilities, improved relationships and spiritual deepening, all of which follow tragedy." The paradox of trauma is that loss and gain both happen, grief and gratitude both happen, vulnerability and strength both happen.

Another ancient wisdom revealed is that emotional consequences do not arise from the adversity, but from your beliefs about the adversity. Fortunately, those beliefs are malleable.

"Flourishing" can be seen as the mental equivalent of Dr. Attia's physical prescription in "Outlive" (Chapter 80) for a longer and a better life. Tying the two together, Seligman writes: "Psychology and medicine, following Freud and the medical model, view the world through the lens of pathology and look only at the toxic effects of malign events. Psychology and medicine get turned on their heads when we ask about the opposite of pathology: about the strengthening effects of benevolent events. Indeed, any endeavor – nutrition, the immune system, welfare, politics, education or ethics – that is fixated on the remedial misses this insight and does half the job: correcting deficits while failing to build strength."

Seligman finds that optimists bounce back quickly from setbacks, thinking "It's going away quickly. I can do something about it and its just this one situation." Pessimists do not bounce back from defeat, thinking "It's going to last forever, it's going to undermine everything and there's nothing I can do about it."

Fortunately, Seligman teaches that optimism can be learned and that learning is invaluable. "Pessimists get depressed much more readily than optimists, they underachieve in their jobs, in the classroom and on the sports field, and their relationships are rockier."

Not surprisingly, the book finds that pessimism and optimism, "the great amplifiers of learned helplessness and mastery" greatly affects health and longevity.

We learn that optimists are less vulnerable to disease because they (1) have healthier lifestyles (2) act on medical advice readily (3) are more likely to watch their weight (4) don't smoke (5) exercise (6) sleep better, and (7) have more friends and more love in their life.

As the author says, "misery may love company, but company does not love misery, and the ensuring loneliness of pessimists may be a path to illness."

Perhaps the bottom line to all of this is the simple prescription that to change your life you have to change your thinking. Today we have the knowledge and the resources to allow each one of us to markedly improve our lives and well-being.

83

The Scourge of Ageism

Your writer was surprised by the findings of ageism expert Becca Levy, in her book "Breaking the Age Code," that your beliefs about aging determine how long and well you live.

Why do the Japanese live longer and enjoy old age so much more than us? They simply treat old age as something to enjoy, and they are respected by others. In America, the media and the "youthfulness industry" treat it as something to be feared and resented, like some sort of dreaded disease. Age beliefs, it turns out, add or steal nearly eight years to your life. Our culture sets up scripts that we subconsciously act out.

The prevailing negative age stereotypes in our culture don't just color how others act towards older adults, it greatly affects how they see themselves and how they act. In other words, your aging beliefs impact your health psychologically, biologically and behaviorally.

It is important for older adults to "flip the script" since, as Carl Jung observed, "Until you make the unconscious conscious, it will direct your life and you will call it fate." The author notes that people with negative age beliefs suffer from lower self-esteem, take fewer prescribed medications and exercise less, creating a self-fulfilling prophecy.

The medical profession gets called out for its failure to treat many conditions in older adults that they would readily treat in younger persons. When an 85 year old was told by his doctor that his ailing knee was normal for an 85 year old, the patient replied, "But my other knee is 85 years old too, and it doesn't hurt one bit."

Why is dementia five times more common in the U.S. than in India? "In India, older individuals are treated with great respect and routinely sought out for counsel on everything from financial investments to family conflicts," writes Levy. Failure to be cared for and integrated into the community causes that portion of the brain responsible for memory to shrink three times faster. Even among persons with the Alzheimer's gene, there is almost a 50% less chance of developing the disease for those with positive age beliefs.

The concept that life is worth living, that we have purpose and are useful makes a huge difference in longevity -- including making us more likely to engage in healthy behaviors -- and contributes to a "compression of morbidity" or the number of unhealthy years.

Ageism is a dated prejudice that is ripe for elimination. It no longer reflects the reality of aging today. As James Baldwin said,

"Not everything that's faced can be changed, but nothing can be changed until it is faced."

APPENDIX:
ABOUT ETTINGER LAW FIRM

1

The Ettinger Elder Law Estate Planning Process

So many people are afraid to go and see a lawyer for estate planning. And for good reason! They may not want to look foolish, knowing so little about the subject. They may feel intimidated by the knowledge and authority of the attorney. They are frightened about the cost or of being taken advantage of. They may have had a bad previous experience with a lawyer, either in the same or in another field of law, and so on.

For this reason, we start with the premise that we must first build the client's confidence. We do this by offering a free initial consultation where we explore the client's social and financial issues. It's often like chatting with someone in their living room. We like to get to know you and your overall situation. It's a low-key, judgment-free zone. We park our egos at the door when we come in and endeavor to treat our clients as the peers and equals they are.

Next up, we review the client's current documents to see if they are still legally valid and personally valid -- in other words are these still the people you want in charge and is this still the way you want to leave your estate. Following, we review the client's personal and financial situation, and then make our recommendations as to what we feel the client should do and quote a fee. We then give the client a copy of our book "Ettinger Law Firm's Guide to Protecting Your Future" and advise them which chapters apply to them and their family, For those who prefer to watch video, we direct them to our 37 minute estate planning video on the homepage of our website, trustlaw.com.

You, the client, are invited back for a second free consultation in two or three weeks to have any questions answered that you may have from the initial consultation and from the chapters you read. Then we draft the estate plan together with you by asking who you wish to have in charge for legal and financial matters, who do you want to make medical decisions for you and how would you like to leave your estate -- all at once or over a period of time, equal or unequal amounts, etc. At the same time we provide you with feedback by the way of options and ideas.

At the end of the second meeting we have usually gotten to the point where we feel that you fully understand the plan and then provide you with a three page proposal outlining the work to be done, the benefits, the cost and the terms of payment.

Appendix: About Ettinger Law Firm

Unique among elder law estate planning firms, we do not have the client sign a Fee Agreement, or pay a retainer fee as is the standard. Instead, we provide a Fee Proposal which states that we will prepare all the documents at your request. We ask that you come in for a third meeting to review all the documents and, once all have been executed and you are satisfied, you pay at the end. However, our proposal states that until you complete the matter you have no obligation to the law firm.

Our thinking is this. If you, the client, are in control of the process the whole time then it's the best place for you to be. If we're here to serve you, and it's the best place for you to be, then we feel it's the best place for us to be.

Once you become a client we will contact you every three years to come in for a free review. The review makes sure your plan is up to date both personally and legally so that it works when you need it -- not when you wrote it perhaps decades earlier.

We also send you our weekly law letter, The Ettinger Elder Elert, to further help keep you and your plan current.

2

Features of Our Practice

1. **Experience.** Over thirty-three years practicing exclusively Elder Law Estate Planning.

2. **Knowledge.** Authored the treatise "Ettinger Law Firm's Guide to Protecting Your Future" updated annually. Complimentary copy given to each client at initial consultation.

3. **Comfort.** Low key approach. Clients are advised when it may be better to wait or if their current plan is adequate.

4. **Service.** Serviced over thirty thousand satisfied clients since 1991. We charge fees based on our knowledge and experience of the work required to address our client's needs.

5. **Oversight.** Principal attorney Michael Ettinger was admitted to the New York Bar in 1980, is the Past President of The American Association of Trust, Estate, and Elder Law Attorneys and was a Founding Member of The American Academy of Estate Planning Attorneys.

6. **Comprehensive.** Ettinger clients have effective plans for disability instead of just estate or death planning alone. Thousands of successful Medicaid cases filed.

7. **Continuity.** Attorneys on staff in their 20's, 30's, 40's, 50's and 60's to ensure mentoring and continuity of your elder law estate planning firm.

8. **Satisfaction.** Free initial consultation, free follow-up consultation, and no fees payable until the work is completed and you are satisfied.

9. **Systems.** Our trademarked process keeps you up-to-date on law changes and includes a free review every three years for changes in your health, your assets and in your family. An Ettinger plan is designed to work in the future when you need it.

10. **Convenience.** Thirteen offices statewide for your convenience and the convenience of your other family members.

11. **Reviews.** 195 client reviews at trustlaw.com with a 4.9 out of 5 rating.

3

The Ettinger Law Firm Way

Every law firm has a unique culture. Ours is captured in 30 fundamentals we call The Ettinger Law Firm Way. All 30 of these may be found on our website, trustlaw.com, under "Resources".

1. **Do What's Best For The Client.** In all situations, do what's best for the client, even if it's to our own short-term detriment. Put their needs ahead of our own. There's no greater way to build a reputation than to steadfastly do what's right for others.

2. **Share Information.** With appropriate respect for confidentiality, share information freely throughout our organization. The more people know, the better we can collaborate. Learn to ask yourself, "Who else needs to know this?"

3. **Focus on Solutions.** It's easy to point out problems. It's better to identify solutions; but it makes a true difference when you step up and become a part of the solution.

4. **Find A Way.** Take personal responsibility for making things happen. Respond to every situation by looking for how we can do it, rather than explaining why it can't be done. Be resourceful and show initiative. Don't make excuses or wait for others to solve the problem. See issues through to their completion.

5. **Be Positive.** You have the power to choose your attitude. Choose to be joyful, optimistic, and enthusiastic. Give people the benefit of the doubt. Your attitude is contagious. Spread optimism and positive energy.

6. **Collaborate.** Work together. Be open to new ideas and different approaches. Collaboration generates better ideas and solutions than does working alone. Be inclusive.

7. **Look Ahead and Anticipate.** Solve problems before they happen by anticipating future issues, planning for contingencies, and addressing them in advance. Work with appropriate lead times. Preventing issues is always better than fixing them.

8. **"Bring It" Every Day.** Have a passion for what we do and be fully engaged. Make the most of each day by approaching every task with energy, focus, purpose, and enthusiasm. Work with a sense of urgency to get things done.

9. **Work Smart.** Be organized and plan your work for maximum efficiency. Have all the tools and resources necessary before starting

your work. Be thoughtful about your schedule, and have a game plan for your calls, your tasks, and your workday.

10. **Work on Yourself.** Be a lifelong learner. Seek out and take advantage of every opportunity to gain more knowledge, to increase your skills, and to become an expert. Be resourceful about learning and sharing best practices.

11. **Be A Mentor.** The best way to influence others is through your own example. Walk the talk. Take responsibility, both formally and informally, to coach, guide, teach, and mentor others. Be the change you want to see.

12. **Listen Generously.** Listening is more than simply "not speaking". Give others your undivided attention. Be present and engaged. Minimize the distractions and let go of the need to agree or disagree. Suspend your judgment and be curious to know more, rather than jumping to conclusions. Above all, listen to understand.

13. **Think Team First.** It's not about you. Don't let your own ego or personal agenda get in the way of doing what's best for the team. Be there for each other and be willing to step into another role or help a co-worker when that's what's required for success. Help each other to succeed.

14. **Make Quality Personal.** Demonstrate a passion for excellence and take pride in the quality of everything you touch and everything you do. Have a healthy disdain for mediocrity. Good is not good enough. Always ask yourself, "Is this my best work?"

15. **Speak Straight.** Speak honestly in a way that helps to make progress. Say what you mean, and be willing to ask questions, share ideas, or raise issues that may cause conflict when it's necessary for team success. Be transparent and courageous enough to say what needs to be said. Address issues directly with those who are involved or affected.

16. **Honor Commitments.** Do what you say you're going to do, when you say you're going to do it. This includes being on time for all phone calls, appointments, meetings, and promises. If a commitment can't be fulfilled, notify others early and agree on a new deliverable to be honored.

17. **Get Clear On Expectations.** Create clarity and avoid misunderstandings by discussing expectations upfront. Set expectations for others and ask when you're not clear on what they expect of you. End all meetings with clarity about action items, responsibilities, and due dates.

18. **Show Meaningful Appreciation.** Recognizing people doing things right is more effective than pointing out when they do things wrong. Regularly extend meaningful acknowledgement and appreciation – in all directions throughout our organization.

19. **Deliver Effortless Expectations.** Find ways to make working with you/us easier. Provide simple and complete instructions. When in doubt, do more rather than pushing the work back to others in the firm or the client. Streamline our processes. Simplify everything. Be unusually helpful.

20. Walk In Your Clients' Shoes. Understand your clients' world and perspective. Know their challenges and frustrations. The better you understand them, the more effectively you can anticipate and meet their needs.

21. Create A Great Impression. Every conversation, phone call, e-mail, letter, and even voicemail, sets a tone and creates an impression. Pay attention to every interaction and be sure you're setting a tone that's friendly, warm, and helpful.

22. Take Pride In Your Appearance. Your personal appearance makes a strong statement about the pride you take in your performance. Dress neatly and professionally. The appearance of our office takes a similar statement about the quality of our work. Take responsibility to see that our office environment is clean, neat, and professional.

23. Make Healthy Choices. Take care of yourself at home and at the office. Eat well, exercise, and get adequate sleep. Support each other in making healthy choices. The healthier you are, the more you'll thrive personally and professionally.

24. Communicate To Be Understood. Know your audience. Write and speak in a way that they can understand. Avoid using internal lingo, acronyms, and legal jargon. Use the simplest possible explanations.

25. Pay Attention To The Details. Missing just one detail can have an enormous impact on a client. Be a fanatic about accuracy and precision. The goal is to get things right, not simply to get them done. Double-check your work. Get the details right the first time.

26. **Embrace Change and Growth.** What got us here is not the same as what will get us to the next level. Get outside your comfort zone, rather than stubbornly hanging on to old ways of doing things. Embrace change and the possibilities that change and growth bring. Be flexible.

27. **Be Relentless About Improvement.** Regularly reevaluate every aspect of your job to find ways to improve. Don't be satisfied with the status quo. "Because I was taught that way" is not a reason. Guard against complacency. Find ways to get things done better, faster, and more efficiently.

28. **Treasure, Protect and Promote Our Reputation.** We're all responsible for, and benefit from, the Ettinger Law Firm image and reputation. Consider how your actions affect our collective reputation, and be a proud ambassador for the firm.

29. **Go The Extra Mile.** Be willing to do whatever it takes to accomplish the job ... plus a little bit more. Whether it's starting early, staying late, or doing something that's not in your job description, it's the extra mile that separates the ordinary from the extraordinary.

30. **Keep Things Fun.** While our passion for excellence is real, remember that the world has bigger problems than the daily challenges that make up our work. Stuff happens. Keep perspective. Don't take things personally or take yourself too seriously.

Made in the USA
Middletown, DE
23 November 2023

43260372R00176